The Danger Zone

Lost in the Growth Transition

Library of Congress Cataloging-in-Publication
Data is available upon request.

ISBN 978-0-9886932-6-5

First Edition, June 2006
Fourth Edition, October 2019

www.b2bcfo.com

Dedication

Larry Checketts

Christine

Prelude

"Nothing in the world can take the place of persistence. Talent will not; nothing is more common than unsuccessful individuals with talent. Genius will not; unrewarded genius is almost a proverb. Education will not; the world is full of educated derelicts. Persistence and determination alone are omnipotent." [1]

Calvin Coolidge, 30th U.S. President

"All achievements, whether in the business, intellectual, or spiritual world, are the result of definitely directed thought, are governed by the same law and are of the same method; the only difference lies in the object of attainment.

He who would accomplish little must sacrifice little. He who would achieve much must sacrifice much. He who would attain highly must sacrifice greatly." [2]

James Allen

CONTENTS

Dear Business Owner:

This is an open letter to the risk-takers of our society—the owners of privately held growth companies. You are the reason our economic society works. The free enterprise system of the USA would collapse, along with tens of thousands of jobs.

Most of you feel the truthfulness of the adage, "It's lonely at the top." You sometimes wonder if anyone will ever understand you, your goals, your business wishes and ambitions. You also have frustrations that cause you to worry about your business. Some of these worries are with you 24/7/365.

Many of your peers have expressed sentiments such as, "I do not understand why I had more cash when my company's sales were much lower than they are today. I do not understand why bankers will not lend the money I need. I used to love my business when I first started, but now I feel trapped. I don't have time to leave the office to spend time with customers or my family," and so forth.

Expressions similar to the above are symptoms of a larger problem, a phenomenon called **The Danger Zone**. The purpose of this book, titled *The Danger Zone, Lost in the Growth Transition*, is to help you understand this phenomenon and to give some suggestions on how to avoid or get out of this situation.

The goal of this book will have been accomplished if it helps one business owner.

Hopefully, it will help many.

Sincerely,

Jerry L. Mills

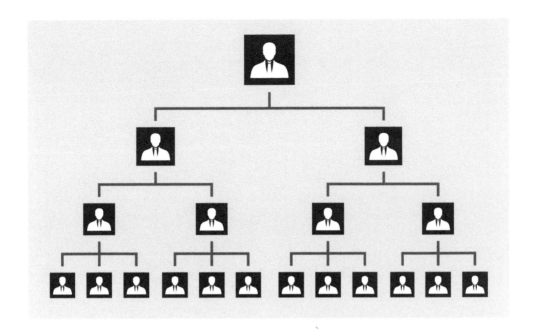

CHAPTER 1

The Unofficial Organization of Your Company

Let's start this book by sharing some information that I have learned from decades of working with the owners of privately held companies. They don't teach this in college. Your understanding of this information should assist you in the future as your company grows.

Some authors have attempted to explain these subjects, but none have done so in the concise manner that you will see here.

Excluded from this book is unrealistic idealism. I share these experiences as your peer, with the hope you will avoid the pain of reinventing the wheel. Business "pioneers" have already paved the way for us to avoid certain pitfalls and to meet our goals more efficiently.

The learned authors who write popular books will tell you that you need two things to be successful in your company: a mission statement and an organizational chart. It's difficult to argue with the logic of these PhDs and learned people. However, the subject matter can become complex, and there are more solutions than just these two ideas.

Mission Statement

Mission Statements

When I began this business, I assumed that I would need to help my clients prepare a mission statement. That was, after all, what the learned authors taught in their popular business books. I quickly found that trying to get a business owner to create a mission statement was harder to do than to get one of my teenagers to clean up their bedroom.

I am a fan of well-written mission statements. There is nothing wrong with the logic of a mission statement, but such statements typically do not work for the owners of privately held companies. There are a variety of reasons why they do not work; the major reason is business owners feel constrained by a mission statement.

Why would a mission statement be confining to a business owner? Dr. Stephen R. Covey discloses a major hurdle for owners of privately held companies on this subject:

> "One of the most important thrusts of my work with organizations is to assist them in developing effective mission statements. And to be effective, that statement has to come from within the bowels of the organization. Everyone should participate in a meaningful way-not just the top strategy planners, but everyone. Once again, the involvement process is as important as the written product and is the key to its use."[3]

Dr. Covey exposes both the solution and the problem in the above paragraph. The problem is owners of privately held companies do not like involving everyone in their company in such an exercise. They know that a company is driven by leaders, not by committees. They like to have control over their business and do not appreciate consultants trying to push them toward a position they do not want to take. Boxing a business owner into a corner with a mission statement can be counter-productive.

People looking in from the outside of a privately held business tend to judge the business owner by the look and feel of the "main" business. This is without understanding that the business owner often has created, or is in the process of creating, other companies that they may not want to disclose until the proper time.

An outside consultant might spend a significant amount of time helping a business owner create a mission statement. The consultant will then charge a lot of money and say, "The job is done."

The job is not done because the mission statement most likely does not fit the other businesses the owner is going to create. In fact, the mission statement may conflict with the other businesses or the future vision the owner has of the company. The new mission statement is then viewed as restrictive to the business owner. Too often, the mission statement becomes an impediment to the entrepreneur. I endorse the sentiment expressed by Collins and Porras in their book, *Built to Last,* which states:

> "Creating a (mission) statement can be a helpful step in building a visionary company, but is only one of thousands of steps in a never ending process..." [4]

Core Values or Mission Statements?

Entrepreneurs may have a better chance of improving their business by defining core values than solely by writing mission statements. Permanent core values should outlast mission statements, which are often ever-changing. Core values of a business are like the foundation of a building that has the ability to add other stories or rooms without changing its foundation.

Core values are defined by James C. Collins and Jerry I. Porras as:

> "The organization's essential and enduring tenets—a small set of general guiding principles; not to be confused with specific cultural or operational practices; not to be compromised for financial gain or short-term expediency." [5]

Some core values that we often see are:

- Honesty and ethics
- Hard work
- Integrity
- Superior customer service

What are the right core values?

There is not a list of core values that will fit into every organization. Rather, core values must come from your inner-most beliefs and desires. Core values are not a marketing position statement that will shift with the tide. The experts on this subject have said the following:

> "When articulating and codifying core ideology, the key step is to capture what is authentically believed, not what other companies set as their values or what the outside world thinks the ideology should be.
>
> In a visionary company, the core values need no rational or external justification. Nor do they sway with the trends and the fads of the day. Nor even do they shift in response to changing market conditions.
>
> Visionary companies tend to have only a few core values, usually between three and six. In fact, we found none of the visionary companies to have more than six core values, and most have less.

And, indeed, we should expect this, for only a few values can be truly core—values so fundamental and deeply held that they will change or be compromised seldom, if ever." [6]

Display Your Core Values

One can't teach core values in a business environment. People are either honest or they are not. They most likely learned this honesty or dishonesty at a young age, and there is nothing we can to do to change their core values. People either have a good work ethic or they do not. People desire either to improve the company or work in a company for their own selfish purposes.

> **B2B Adage**: *You can't teach values to employees but you can find people who share your core values.*

You might consider writing down three to six core values that you envision for your company. Post this list in visible places in your business, perhaps even on your website. Then you can begin to hire people (employees, attorneys, accountants, bankers, etc.) who share your core values.

Hold on to Your Core Values

Core values should not shift with the tides of change in a business, as evidenced by the following words of wisdom:

> "Enduring great companies preserve their core values and purpose while their business strategies and operating practices endlessly adapt to a changing world. This is the magical combination of '"preserve the core and stimulate progress.'" [7]

Employee Skills vs. Core Values

Should a business owner hire a skilled person even if this person does not share the core values of the company or the owner?

This is a tough subject for business owners. Naturally, business owners tend to hire people because they have skills. Hiring people without communicating core values can become frustrating for both the person being hired and the company that does the hiring.

> "Myth: Visionary companies are great places to work, for everyone.
>
> Only those who 'fit' extremely well with the core ideology and demanding standards of a visionary company will find it a great place to work. If you go to work for a visionary company, you will either fit and flourish—probably couldn't be happier—or you will likely be expunged like a virus. It's binary. There's no middle ground. It's almost cult-like. Visionary companies are so clear about what they stand for and what they're trying to achieve that they simply don't have room for those unwilling or unable to fit their exacting standards." [8]

There is a different way to look at this concept. Have you ever been in a situation where you were wearing dirty clothes and then accidentally found yourself with a group of people who were well dressed? If you have not been in this situation, then imagine how you would feel. Of course you would most definitely feel out of place. You would feel self-conscious and would try to get away from that group of people as soon as possible.

This is how it goes with core values. Let's say you have a core value of honesty. You hire people who are honest. This honesty is not only in their hearts, but it is a part of their being. These people enjoy working with others who share this philosophy.

Let's imagine you hire another person who is dishonest. What is going to happen in this situation? The outcome is predictable: the honest people will feel uncomfortable around the dishonest person. Things will be said behind this person's back such as, "Why do you think the owner hired him?" The dishonest person will try to fit in, but the other employees won't allow this to happen. They might not say anything to the owner (this is to protect their job security), but they will not socialize with or trust this person. This would be tantamount to trying to mix water and oil.

> **B2B Adage**: *You want to get rid of anyone in your organization who does not share your core values. They should already have learned core values, such as honesty and good work ethic before joining your company.*

Let's create a situation about core values, simply as an example. Imagine that you adopt one of the core ideologies of Motorola:

"Treat each employee with dignity, as an individual." [9]

This sounds easy, doesn't it? What qualities would a company need to have to treat each employee with dignity? A few words come to mind: fairness, composure, restraint, kindness, wisdom, etc. Let's select just one word from the preceding list: *composure*.

What does it take to embrace composure as a core value? What are the rewards that follow a person who achieves composure in business dealings with others? James Allen wrote the following words about this subject in the early 1900s in his book, *As a Man Thinketh*:

> "The calm man, having learned how to govern himself, knows how to adapt himself to others; and they, in turn, reverence his spiritual strength, and feel that they can learn of him and rely upon him. The more tranquil a man becomes,

the greater his success, his influence, his power for good. Even the ordinary trader will find his business prosperity increase as he develops a greater self-control and equanimity, for people will always prefer to deal with a man whose demeanor is strongly equitable."[10]

What are your personal core values? What are the core values of your company? Your company might benefit by documenting and promoting these values. Viewing this subject in the big picture, good core values are a type of a mission statement.

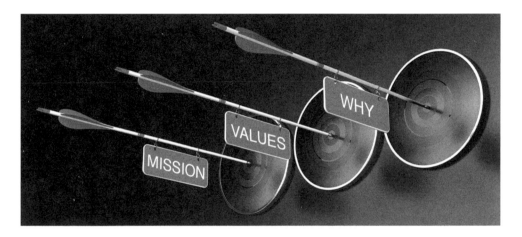

Start with Why

Simon Sinek is one of the great thought leaders of our time. His book, *Start with Why* is profound in its teachings and makes an insightful statement:

> "Very few people or companies can clearly articulate WHY they do WHAT they do. When I say WHY, I don't mean to make money—that is a result. By WHY, I mean what is your purpose, cause, or belief? WHY does your company exist? WHY do you get out of bed in the morning? And WHY should anyone care?" [11]

The above is a gut-punch and an indictment against any company or (healthy) person that works in the U.S. economy and can't easily articulate why they get out of bed each morning and why anyone should care.

It must be a frustrating life without a purpose, cause, belief or without the ability to easily express these attributes. These attributes are significant and are defined as follows:

Purpose: The reason something is done or created

Cause: A principle, aim or movement that, because of a deep commitment, one is prepared to defend

Belief: Trust or confidence in someone or something

Simon Sinek gave an example of the "Why Statement" of Apple, one of the most successful companies in the history of the United States of America:

> "Everything we do, we believe in challenging the status quo. We believe in thinking differently.
>
> The way we challenge the status quo is by making our products beautifully designed, simple to use and user-friendly.
>
> And we happen to make great computers.
>
> Wanna buy one?" [12]

Our company decided to use Apple's Why Statement as a format for ours, which reads:

> "In everything we do, we believe in improving the lives of business owners.
>
> We believe each owner is unique and important to our society.
>
> The way we improve their lives is by understanding their goals and by removing barriers that get in the way.
>
> We have unique talent, tools and processes."

We easily combined our Why Statement with our core values of honesty, integrity and objectivity. This process has allowed us to do four things:

1. Easily explain to our current and future clients why it is important to them that everyone in our company should get out of bed each morning.

2. Communicate the same to those who serve these owners, such as bankers, attorneys, wealth manages, insurance agencies, investment bankers, M&A firms, etc.

3. Attract people to our company who share the same Why and core values.

4. Repel people from our company who do not share the same Why and core values.

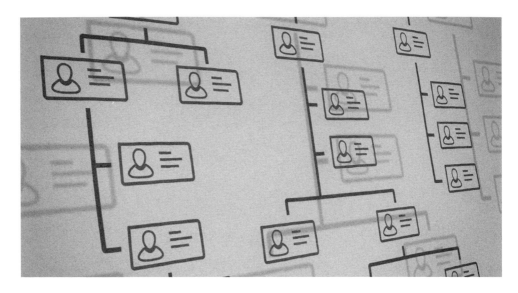

Why Organizational Charts Don't Always Work

Let's look at another subject which got my knuckles rapped many times before I learned a tough lesson.

It took me about a decade to figure out why owners of privately held companies do not like organizational charts. This was frustrating to me! In many instances I felt I had failed my clients. After all, the experts who write popular books preach that a company needs to have such a document to succeed.

I tried in vain to follow that advice. After many failures, I have concluded that owners of privately held companies will rarely use an organizational chart, regardless of the number of times they are implored to use one. There are numerous reasons business owners do not like organization charts, a few being:

1. They fear that managers and supervisors will ask for pay raises if they see they are on an "equal level" with other managers or supervisors on the chart.

2. The organization of the company is constantly changing which makes it difficult for a company to have an accurate and current organizational chart.

3. Some business owners are good at delegating responsibility but sometimes have difficulty delegating authority, thus the organizational chart is often rendered useless.

   B2B Adage: *If you delegate responsibility without the authority, you will after a period of time, be given back the responsibility.*

4. Business owners like to talk to employees outside the boundaries of an organizational chart.

5. The business owners fear that some employees will not perform duties that are not included in the organizational chart. The fear is that an employee might say, "That is not my responsibility."

6. The organization chart does not typically allow consideration of other wholly owned entities that might be smaller than the largest entity.

7. Overall, it is a confining document to the business owner. Some owners would prefer to wear a straitjacket than use an organizational chart.

I am not saying that I like horizontal delegation of duties. Conversely, I strongly believe in the process of delegation of authority and responsibility through managers and supervisors.

On the other hand, the business belongs to the business owner. The owner has the right to talk to anyone in the company, regardless of a formal chain of command.

We will discuss the topic of delegating responsibility and authority in a subsequent chapter. For now, we can safely conclude that the typical organizational chart will not work for some owners of privately held companies. There is, however, a very simple alternative to creating a formal organizational chart that does not take much effort to document. The beauty of the following is that everyone in your company will understand it immediately and will not question its logic.

The Unofficial Organizational Chart

Each company owned by an entrepreneur has an unofficial organizational chart. This organizational chart is often created by default—it merely happens as an organization evolves and changes. The future success of the company is predicated upon how well this organizational chart functions. The unofficial organizational chart looks like this:

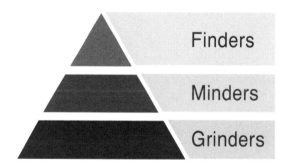

B2B Adage: *Whether written or unwritten, the company's organizational chart exists today. The Finder's future success is dependent upon working properly within the rules of the informal organizational chart.*

There is helpful documentation about the roles of *Finders, Minders and Grinders* in subsequent chapters.[13] It's important to understand this informal organization of your company. The key to making this organizational chart work is the Finder. The organization will function well if Finders perform their duties properly.

The organizational chart of the company that is headed for **The Danger Zone** looks like the following:

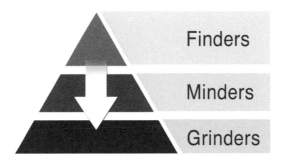

The objective of this book is to do the following with the above organizational chart:

B2B Adage: *Every company has an unofficial organizational chart, which is intentionally or unintentionally created by the business owner.*

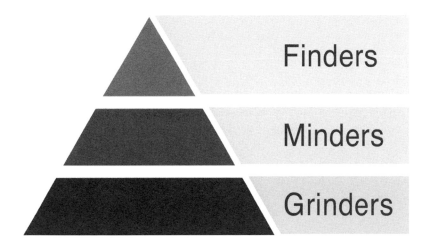

CHAPTER 2
Entrepreneurs are Finders

Entrepreneurs are different from everyone else in our society. They are unique among all individuals. Very few people ever discover what inspires them to do amazing things. Very few people appreciate their intelligence, drive, and dare I say, love for their fellow human beings.

They typically have an above-average IQ, even though most of them are reluctant to admit this. Many successful owners have dropped out of high school or college to start their businesses. Some are embarrassed to say they only have a high school education, even though they are brilliant and employ hundreds, even thousands of people. Some owners simply did not need the formality of a diploma to succeed.

I call entrepreneurs "the geniuses of our society." They are fun to be around. Their enthusiasm for life and others is infectious. It's as if their minds never quit working. Their passion for life is inspiring.

Entrepreneurs usually have highly ethical core values. Most of them are also very creative.

Contrary to one myth, most of them don't do what they do "just for the money." Contrary to another myth, they typically care deeply about their employees and associates. Their heart often aches with the personal tragedies of their employees, although many entrepreneurs do not always openly show their feelings.

It's Lonely at the Top

Entrepreneurs live in the future and are risk-takers. They will risk their money and time to make a difference in the future. The future is all that matters to entrepreneurs! This is one of the things that distinguishes them from everyone else. While the employees may have fleeting thoughts about their company's future, they functionally live in either the past or the present.

One thing that often frustrates entrepreneurs is the realization that they alone are concerned about the future of their company. This is one of the reasons for the adage, "It is lonely at the top." It truly is a very lonely spot, but it is really the only place to be for those of us who are true entrepreneurs.

Entrepreneurs need to realize that, with few exceptions, nobody will ever really understand or empathize with their loneliness. One may meet an owner and say, "I understand how you feel." The person making the statement may have good intentions, but the statement is naive.

> **B2B Adage:** *It is lonely at the top. Don't expect anyone to understand or fully empathize with that loneliness.*

They Pull People into the Future

Entrepreneurs spend a significant amount of their time and energy pulling people into the future. They will hold meetings and retreats, write memos, emails, and use other methods to try to express their visions and ideas. In frustration, they will sometimes say to themselves, "Does anyone ever listen or care?"

The answer is yes, they will listen, but they will not understand. They may understand a part of the vision, but they will never understand the "big picture" that entrepreneurs have. They do not understand the risk the owner takes nor the reason for the risk-taking.

They do not understand the entrepreneurs' need to create and succeed.

Life Time Zones

The employees, and most people by whom the entrepreneur is surrounded, live in different time zones than the entrepreneur. This doesn't mean Mountain Standard Time (MST) vs. Eastern Standard Time (EST). Rather, this refers to "life time zones" that are just as different as MST vs. EST, and are easy to distinguish once entrepreneurs understand the concept of life time zones within individuals.

Knowledge is power. It is important for the entrepreneur to understand this concept as illustrated in the following table.

Life Time Zone	Common Reference	B2B Reference
Future	Entrepreneur	Finder
Past	Managers or Administration	Minder
Present	Technicians or Laborers	Grinder

The remainder of this book will refer to entrepreneurs and business owners as *Finders*, which is a more accurate description of their function within the organization. The teachings of this book will go into some detail on Minders and Grinders in an effort to help Finders avoid ***The Danger Zone***.

Finders are very different from Minders and Grinders. We can thank our Maker that they were born that way; otherwise, the future of economic society would be very bleak.

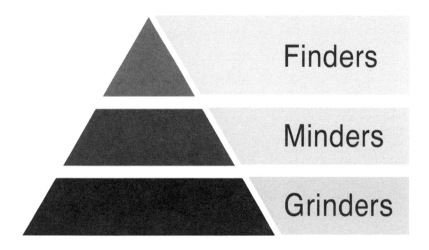

CHAPTER 3
Finders Live in the Future

This chapter will explain some of the basic concepts of the role of the Finder in the company organization.

Finders are the leaders of the company. They are not necessarily the people who lead all company employees on a daily basis.
Finders demonstrate the type of leadership that "pulls" people into the future—employees, current customers and future customers.

> **B2B Adage**: *Finders live in the future with little regard to what has happened in the past.*

Let's identify who is not a Finder. A salesperson, a company's sales force and the people who manufacture the company's widgets are not Finders. These people are Grinders, which is discussed in a subsequent chapter.

Finders demonstrate some specific attributes that are essential to success. There are numerous terms that can describe the leadership of a Finder, such as:

- Visionary
- Idea generator
- Innovator or dreamer
- Catalyst for future change
- Relationship builder or creator

Note that all of the above attributes or functions require future action. Finders are all about the future. They do not live in the past. They view the past as a tool from which to learn, not as a place in which to dwell.

This concept of the future thinking of Finders took me many years to understand. The first time this came to my attention was when I was working in public accounting.

Our clients would pay significant amounts of money for audits and other types of services that were mostly historical in nature. I found it odd that the Finders would spend so much money for these services but, simultaneously, show little interest in what we were doing. Finally, out of curiosity, I gathered enough courage to ask a Finder why he was not interested in what my colleagues and I were doing. "After all," I said, "you are paying a lot of money for this information." He looked at me and quietly said, "Today is Wednesday. I have 75 employees. At this moment I'm very worried about making my next payroll, which is two days from today. I honestly don't know where I will get the money to pay my 75 employees on Friday morning." He then looked away from me and totally ignored me. That was a significant moment for me in my understanding of Finders. As I sat there in front of this good man, I pondered what he might do if he could not pay his people on the next payday. Suddenly, my concerns about what I felt was important to this Finder regarding the historical audit of his company's financial statements seemed trivial.

That experience instilled in me a desire to learn so that I could eventually help Finders with whatever concerns they might have, especially if they were critical, such as making the next payroll.

The Beginning Is All about Finding

Finders start their businesses for countless reasons. They typically have a passion and find that starting a business is often the only way to satisfy that passion. They will take significant risks to fulfill the passion that drives them 24/7/365.

There is usually one constant at the start of a business. Finders spend most of their time in "Finding activities." They will work almost 24/7/365 for long periods of time in these Finding activities, which usually consist of:

- Building relationships with future and current customers
- Creating relationships with vendors, bankers and lenders
- Delegating tasks to employees or associates
- Causing sales to increase and cash to come into the company

Mostly Relationship Building

The Finding activities on the previous page have one thing in common: they all are mostly about the Finder creating relationships with others.

A good Finder spends most of his or her time building relationships and "pulling" others into the Finder's future. The success of any company is due to the relationships that the Finder is able to make with others. *Building relationships takes time* and is typically the best time the Finder can spend in helping the company succeed. Show me a good Finder who will spend 30 to 40 hours a week in Finding activities and I will show you a company that has a high degree of probability of success in the future.

Conversely, show me a Finder who stops spending time in Finding activities, and I will show you a company that is starting an inevitable cycle toward financial trouble.

B2B Adage: *Successful Finders are good relationship builders.*

As a Finder, one should consider understanding *Minding* and *Grinding* in order to avoid being caught up in such activities. We are going to spend some time talking about those activities and what they entail in the following chapters of this book.

Finding the Right Direction

A major role for the Finder is to make sure the company is going in the right direction. Competition and the market may cause the Finder to quickly determine that the company is going in the wrong direction and that a course correction is necessary.

Stephen R. Covey wrote about this subject. He quotes Peter Drucker and Warren Bennis:

> "Management is doing things right; leadership is doing the right things." [14]

Dr. Covey told an interesting story in his book regarding the differences between management and leadership:

> "You can quickly grasp the important difference between the two if you envision a group of producers cutting their way through the jungle with machetes. They're the producers, the problem solvers. They're cutting through the undergrowth, clearing it out.
>
> The managers are behind them, sharpening their machetes, writing policy and procedure manuals, holding muscle development programs, bringing in improved technologies and setting up working schedules and compensation programs for machete wielders.
>
> The leader is the one who climbs the tallest tree, surveys the entire situation and yells, 'Wrong jungle!'
>
> But how do the busy, efficient producers and managers often respond? 'Shut up! We're making progress.'
>
> As individuals, groups, and businesses, we're often so busy cutting through the undergrowth we don't even realize we're in the wrong jungle."[15]

A Finder's role is to make sure the business is in the right jungle and to have the courage to change course when needed.

B2B Adage: *Finders evoke strong emotions from others, such as love or hate. There is no reason to try to be friends with everyone, because they are looking for a leader, not a friend.*

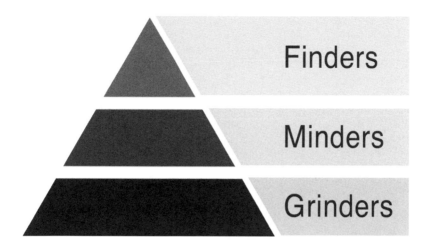

CHAPTER 4
Minders Live in the Past

Minders are critical to the company's success: the company will not survive without good Minders. One can appreciate both their intelligence and their desire to help the Finder. Most Minders are very loyal to the owner. They are typically very honest and ethical in their business dealings.

Minders are the key administrative people of the company. A Minder may be the company's controller, bookkeeper, accounting manager, or IT Manager.

Minding activities are necessary for the success of any company.

Therefore, hiring, training and retaining good Minders is critical for the future success of the company.

> **B2B Adage**: *Minders live in the past and are not future thinkers.*

Most of the assignments given to Minders deal with matters or events that have happened in the past, such as:

1. Historical financial statements
2. Last month's sales tax return
3. Last month's bank reconciliation
4. Proper document filing
5. Making copies of information for bankers
6. Fixing non-functional software systems
7. Installing software and converting old data

All of the above items need to be done and to be done correctly.

Finders simply need to be aware that it is often difficult for Minders to be concerned about something that might happen a year or two in the future when they are working to try to finish documenting things that have been done in the past. It's impossible for the mind to be in two different time zones at the same time.

B2B Adage: *Finders are not good Minders.*

Finders typically do not have the accounting, IT or other background to work extensively in Minding activities. By nature, Finders detest this work. They resent the fact that they have to spend their time in countless meetings, working on cash flow, hiring and firing people, or meeting with accountants, attorneys and bankers.

Common Mistakes

Finders often unintentionally make mistakes regarding their Minders. Some of these mistakes stem from the Finder misunderstanding the life time zone difference between a Finder and a Minder. Finders often like to talk with the Minder about the future of the company. Finders do not always understand that Minders are not interested in future thinking.

Minders need to be led by the Finder or by others. There is nothing wrong with the need to be led; it is the natural order of things in a business.

Minders are very practical and logical. They do not like *rah-rah* leading from Finders. They like facts. They do not like to be told a story they can't believe.

Below are some ideas that will help Finders with their relationship with Minders:

- Meet on a regular basis with your Minders to establish the priorities. Ask them what they are working on and what they feel are their priorities for the next few weeks. Listen. You may not always understand why they have certain priorities. If this is the case, ask why they have set these priorities. Express why you may agree or disagree with the priorities. It is always best to have the Finder and the Minder agree on priorities. Ultimately, the Minder must follow the priorities assigned by the Finder.

- Minders do not like the stress of a company's tight cash situations. There is nothing wrong with this and a Finder should not expect a Minder to enjoy going to work each day in a company that does not have cash to pay its bills. Meet often with your Minder if the company's cash is tight. Explain in detail your plan to correct the cash situation. If you do not have a plan, make one by going out and discovering the right people to correct the situation. Do not expect the Minder to fix your company's cash flow problems if they do not have the skills or experience.

- As a company grows, the Minder is often put in a situation where he or she simply does not understand what to do in many accounting or IT situations. As the Finder, be the leader and get a mentor to help teach the Minder. Don't expect a miracle from the Minder if the person simply has not been taught how to take care of all of the situations of a growth company.

- Finders often create more than one company. Levels of complexity are introduced when multiple companies owned by the Finder start doing business together, such as sales, transfers of cash, or payments of loans. These transactions, called "intercompany transactions," are often very complicated and often have implications to the Finder in business, banking, and taxation circumstances. It may not be wise to assume your Minder will understand how to deal with all of these situations. In these situations, a Finder should get a mentor for the Minder.

- Minders are motivated when the Finder sincerely shows appreciation for work well done. A gesture of appreciation, such as a gift certificate for two at a nice restaurant, will go a long way.

- Do not ask your Minder to be a check signer on business accounts. As will be discussed in a later chapter, you are placing this person in a situation to fail and/or to steal from the company.

Minders are critical to your company. As a Finder, realize that your role will most likely be less of a skills teacher and more of a leader to your Minders.

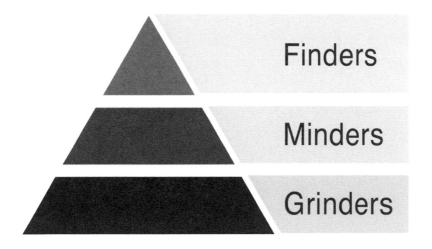

CHAPTER 5

Grinders
Today is all that matters

Grinders are essential for the growth of any company. It is important for a Finder to understand the key attributes of a Grinder. These are the Grinders' preferences:

1. Work only in the present.
2. Do not like to delegate.
3. Often distrust Finders and Minders.
4. Like doing one thing at a time.
5. Will do as instructed, but will rarely generate new ideas.

A Different Time Zone

Grinders work in a different time zone than Finders and Minders. They only care about today. A manufacturing Grinder only cares about the number of widgets to be created each day. A telemarketing Grinder only cares about the number of phone calls to be made today. They give no thought as to what has happened in the company in the past. They are not concerned about the future.

They assume that someone in management will provide the materials or other resources needed to do their jobs tomorrow. They often do not care about the customer.

> **B2B Adage**: *Grinders are only concerned about what happens today. No concern is given about the past or the future.*

Their goal is to get through today, go home, have a pizza, and go bowling or watch television. There is no worry about tomorrow for the Grinder.

Grinders often have distrust for Finders and Minders. If you call a company meeting, one of the first things the Grinder will think is, "What are they going to take away from me today?" They frequently think that Finders and Minders are working against them by wanting to deny them raises, health benefits, profit-sharing, or other such items. They will often bolt from the company if they are offered a little more money from a competitor.

This book will not spend a lot of time on Grinders because Finders usually understand how Grinders do their work. Finders also usually know how to motivate and train Grinders.

Finders, however, often find it difficult to understand why Grinders sometimes distrust them. It is a fact of life—just don't take it personally. Your job as a Finder, as it relates to Grinders, is to deliver your product or service at the lowest possible cost. This may mean that you may not give pay raises in the future. This may mean that you may be forced to cut back on healthcare or other benefits in order to be competitive.

That is your job and that is one of the reasons it's lonely at the top.

SALES
CASH

CHAPTER 6
Where does the cash go?

Two frustrated business owners interviewed us at their corporate office a few years ago. They had previously interviewed five other consulting firms and could not get an answer to their questions. They asked us, "Why did we have more operating cash in the bank when we were at $20MM in sales than we have today at $60MM in sales? **Where does the cash go**?"

The answer to their questions took us about two hours to discover. The company had grown in sales to the point where it had more than $10MM in trade receivables. Conversely, the bank line of credit had not increased over the years and was fixed at $1MM in borrowing capacity.

To make matters more difficult, the customers that owed the combined $10MM were very large companies that paid about one hundred days after the invoice date. Meanwhile, their vendors wanted payment in about 30 days. Payroll to their 400+ employees was due weekly.

The company's cash was tied up in trade receivables and the company was in danger of running completely out of operational cash. The two owners were about to lose everything. Their 400+ employees were, unknowingly, in danger of losing their jobs.

They needed a bank that would give them significantly more money in working capital to free the cash that was tied up in trade receivables.

This company hired us and had their new multi-million dollar working capital bank loan within 90 days. The company's bottom-line income increased by more than 12% over the following 12 months.

Few things are more frustrating for a business owner than to see their company's cash unexpectedly disappear. Below are a few areas that can take cash out of a company.

Employee Theft

Employees can steal cash and inventory. They can charge personal items on corporate credit cards or report fictitious time on payroll. One of our three proprietary books, *Avoiding The Danger Zone, Business Illusions*, has this shocking statistic.

> "It is estimated that 95% of all (U.S.) businesses experience employee theft and management is seldom aware of the actual extent of the losses or even the existence of theft." [17]

receivables – Short for Ac
Receivables; Debts owed t
company, usually sal

Trade Receivables

The collection of cash from receivables can be delayed or permanently stopped by the way customers run the cash management of their own companies. Some customers may not be credit-worthy to be sold on terms.

A privately held company that lends money to customers on terms often, by default, becomes a bank or a lending institution. The company is lending money to customers without any security collateral for the amount that was loaned to the customer with the creation of the receivable invoice. This kind of situation often causes a company's bankers and lenders to get upset to the point where they pause (or end) their banking or lending.

Inventory

Inventory can become a cash quagmire if the company purchases too much, has obsolete inventory and/or purchases inventory at a cost that exceeds the company's ability to earn the expected gross profit margin.

Inventory can be looked at as "idle cash." A company rarely turns over its inventory in thirty days, the number of days their vendors who sell the inventory require payment on their invoices.

Vehicles & Equipment

It is tempting to purchase big-ticket items like vehicles or equipment with operational cash. After all, it is often inconvenient to ask for money from bankers and lenders. It is sometimes easier to write a check for "just this one purchase." It may be in a company's best interest to use OPM (Other People's Money) to purchase such items and to amortize the debt payments over the expected life of the asset.

Vendors

Vendors may unexpectedly change the terms of payment on their invoices. For example, a vendor may historically have given a company 30 days to pay invoices but may suddenly change the terms to 15 days (or Cash on Delivery), which directly impacts a company's cash flow. Vendors may also take away discounts which may negatively impact both cash flow and the company's net income.

Debt Principal Payments

A company may have principal payments on notes that may not be in alignment with operational cash needs. If so, the notes payable may need to be refinanced in order to improve cash.

Income Taxes

Many privately held companies are pass-through entities (LLCs, LLPs, Partnerships, S-Corporations, etc.). The owners' personal income tax structure may cause cash to be taken out of a company (through distributions) to satisfy the income tax requirements of federal, state and/or local governments.

Cost of Goods Sold

Labor, material, or other costs may begin to increase above the company's KPIs (Key Performance Indicators) and may negatively impact cash.

Administrative Expenses

Administrative expenses may balloon and eat into operational cash. Such expenses can often be compared to the industry KPIs (Key Performance Indicators) to determine if a company is spending too much money.

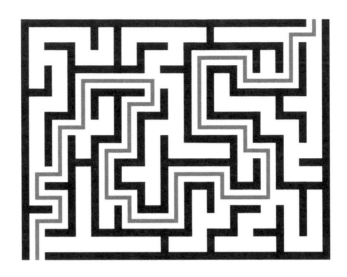

Complexity

Managing a positive operational cash flow can become very complex and may require a certain degree of sophistication. At some point, owners become unable to manage cash in their heads and need help with this critical matter.

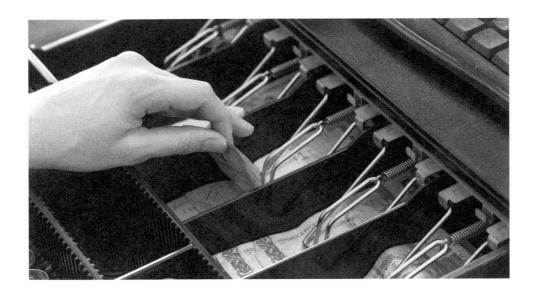

CHAPTER 7

Tempting a Good Person

"[Embezzlers] are diligent and ambitious. They come in early. They are working late. They never take a vacation."[18]

There is too much employee theft in the workplace. Employees steal money, time, inventory, intellectual property and other assets. The following true stories might help educate you on ways that employees steal. First, here is some important information about employee theft:

- 55% of perpetrators are managers.
- 20% of employees are aware of theft in their companies.

- 18 months is the average time it takes an employer to catch a fraud scheme.
- 44% of employees say their companies could do more to reduce fraud.

"I had my own frustrations with upper management but didn't realize it until it was too late. I now see how important it is to have good management—because 55% of employee theft is committed by managers and because the morale and behavior of the remaining 45% is heavily influenced by management style." [19]

A $1,000,000 Theft

We received a phone call a few years ago from a CEO about two weeks after she discovered that her "trusted controller" had stolen a little over $1,000,000 from the company. She was referred to me by an attorney who thought I might be of assistance in trying to salvage the company. The company was a third-generation manufacturing company that employed about 150 people.

The controller, who had stolen the money had left the premises when we were hired, so we learned everything about the theft after she had been terminated.

This was a heart-wrenching experience to witness. The CEO had trusted this controller for nearly a decade. The CEO's trust was demonstrated by giving the controller a lot of responsibilities, but it did not include check signing. Additionally, the company had an independent CPA firm review their financial statements quarterly. These reviews by the CPA firm gave the owner a certain amount of false comfort related to the company's cash and inventory.

The company previously had a $1,000,000 insurance policy for theft and fraud, but the "trusted controller" talked the owner and the insurance company into reducing the insurance by 90% a couple of years before the fraud was detected.

The fraud was simple. The controller forged checks payable to herself in amounts of $6,000 to $8,000 a month for several years. The money was used to fund an illegal drug habit. The bank cashed the forged checks but was able get out of any responsibility for the fraud. The checks were coded to cost of goods sold. There was no "segregation of duties" in the company's internal control system, so the fraud was easy to do and easy to hide from the owner.

The damage to the company from the fraud was too much, and the owner sold the company assets to an out-of-state buyer. Almost all of the 150+ employees lost their jobs because of the company's lack of internal controls that led to the theft.

A third-generation company was killed, not because of any market constraints or competition, but because the company's controller was able to take money that did not belong to her. A company was forced to sell its assets at a discount and 150+ families were damaged in the aftermath—a tragedy beyond words.

A $125,000 Theft

Within a few weeks of being hired by a company we found that the client's finance manager was stealing money. The finance manager had been with the company for some time. We noticed that one particular vendor was listed twice in the company's vendor list. The odd thing about that was the second of the two names of the vendor had a couple of letters transposed.

We found that checks had been written to the name of the vendor with the transposed letters. The checks were written in even amounts each week over a long period of time. Upon further examination, we discovered that these checks were going into the finance manager's personal account. The amount of the theft was about $125,000.

A $250,000 Theft

About three weeks after being hired by a retail company, we became weary of the controller not giving us important bank information. We talked to the owner of the company and were able to obtain copies of the information from the bank.

We had a different employee try to help. We discovered the controller had a three-person scheme to steal from the company. The controller would write a check to one of the company's vendors and hand-deliver the check to a friend. His friend would take the check to a bank teller who would cash the check. The three people (the controller, the friend and the bank teller) would split the cash proceeds.

The thieves were caught by the work performed by my firm. Some relatives of the dishonest controller personally borrowed money and paid the owner back, about $250,000. To our knowledge, the crime was never reported to the authorities.

Theft of Inventory

We were hired by a retail client and noticed that the inventory was shrinking for a certain type of high-dollar merchandise. We double-checked the numbers and helped the company with an inventory count. To our dismay, the merchandise continued to shrink. We created plans with the owner of the company to determine what was causing the inventory shrinkage.

We eventually discovered that a salesperson and the dock manager were stuffing inventory into empty boxes that would be thrown into the company's dumpster during the day. The sales person and the dock manager knew the approximate time the dump truck would stop by each evening to empty the dumpster, which was after the retailer closed the doors to its customers.

The two employees would wait together after the store closed its doors. They would then back up their vehicles to the dumpster, take the merchandise out of the boxes and throw the stolen merchandise into their trunks before the dump truck emptied the dumpster. The thieves were eventually caught. The company was able to catch them due to the implementation of internal controls on inventory shrinkage that my firm recommended.

Credit Card and Check Theft

This was an odd situation, but it shows how creative certain employees can be when stealing from an employer.

A new accounts payable clerk was given the responsibility to cut checks from a pre-approved list. (She was not given the authority to sign the checks.) She cut checks to a credit card company and the checks were signed by the owner. The clerk had a personal credit card with the same credit card company as her employer. The clerk sent the company's check to her credit card company, which deposited the checks and applied them to the clerk's personal credit card account.

The accounts payable clerk became more confident and cut a check to her mother's mortgage company. The check was signed by a hurried business owner who trusted the clerk. The check was sent to the clerk's mother's mortgage company and was cashed.

This embezzlement was discovered by our firm and the clerk was fired. In both cases, internal control measures were not followed by check signers and a devious accounts payable clerk quickly picked up on steps that were skipped by the owners.

Theft of Cash

A non-client had a controller who was trusted by management. She quit her employment for personal reasons. The company hired a new controller without doing a background check.

This was a retail environment in which some customers made some cash purchases. The new controller opened a personal bank account at the company's bank and started taking the company's bank deposits to the bank instead of delegating this duty to others. The controller took the company's cash and put some of the company's money into his personal bank account.

The owners suspected that cash was disappearing from the company, but they couldn't prove it. They hired our firm, and we began looking into the situation. We found it odd that a controller would personally take cash to a bank and suggested the company improve its "segregation of duties." The change in the company's procedures quickly caught the theft. The dishonest controller was fired. The owners did not want to prosecute the thief.

Sometime after firing the dishonest controller the company discovered this person had stolen significant sums of money from previous employers.

> **B2B Adage**: *Far too many white-collar crimes committed by Minders are not reported to the legal authorities, which allows the Minder to steal from future employers.*

A Cashier on Drugs

A retailer hired us to see if we could help with a suspected theft of cash. We discovered the company had seven different cashiers at the registers where customers make payments. Some of the payments were made in cash.

We inquired about the company's employee policy and procedure handbook. The company did not have an HR manual. We suggested to the owner that he quickly hire an attorney who could create such a document. We met with the attorney and the client. We suggested the attorney make sure the new HR manual included specific language about employee drug testing.

The manual was completed and properly delivered and signed by each of the approximate 60 employees.

We advised the owner to begin implementation of the drug testing section of the new HR manual. One of the seven cashiers was a part of the first group of employees tested. The results from the drug testing company arrived in about a week. **The cashier was found to have seven types of illegal drugs in her blood at the time of the drug test**. The attorney was called and the instructions in the HR manual were followed. The employee quickly confessed to the authorities that she had been stealing from the cash registers to fund her illegal drug habits.

B2B Adage: *Every company should have a current Policies and Procedures Employee Handbook. That HR manual should be updated any time a federal, state, or local law or regulation is changed.*

Money Owed to the IRS

We were called into a company shortly after the controller took off with IRS (Internal Revenue Service) money withheld from employees' checks. The controller filed the IRS forms on time and checks were cut by the company to pay taxes. However, the controller did not send the checks to the IRS. Instead, he changed the name on the checks and put the money into his own personal bank account.

To make matters worse, this controller had access to the company's computer file server. Prior to being caught in the theft he stole the hard drive from the file server and left the United States. Unfortunately, the company did not have an off-site backup of the file server.

The IT Department

Can you really say that you know what your IT people are doing with your money? Can you say, with certainty, that your money is being spent wisely on the correct technology? Do you know for a fact that customer lists and other intellectual property are safeguarded?

Typically, the company's IT person does the following:

1. Requests the action
2. Approves the action
3. Executes the action

The above can become problematic:

> "When the same person can request the action, approve the action and then execute it, all of the ingredients are in place for problems.
>
> Businesses face a particularly vexing challenge in preventing fraud by IT "superusers" such as network administrators and senior managers. These individuals may be able to create "ghost" employees, fake vendor accounts or fraudulent purchase orders and invoices." [20]

Nobody who is reputable can guarantee an owner against theft. We can, however, talk about such items as "internal control systems," and "segregation of duties." These terms may seem vague to a Finder, but they are tangible and necessary. Finders, keep in mind that we are not suggesting you need to live in fear, or that you can't trust your key employees.

Business owners, without realizing it, often put employees in a situation where the temptation to steal is simply too great for them to resist.

Ultimately, it is the business owner's fault for putting an employee in a situation that allowed the employee to steal.

> **B2B Adage**: *Some business owners unintentionally place their employees in a position to steal from the company.*

Steal from my own company?

I have witnessed Finders that have put the company's cash into their pockets—from the company's cash registers or other cash sources. I'm not sure why they do this, but I imagine they say something like, "This is my company and my money, and I will use it as I see fit."

The above statement may be true to the business owner; however, Finders who pocket cash (without proper documentation) might find themselves in a situation where the adage comes true: Perception becomes reality.

The employees' perceptions when an owner pockets cash becomes reality to them. I have heard statements from employees such as:

> "The owner is trying to cheat his business partner."

> "The owner is trying to cheat the IRS by taking the cash and not paying income taxes. Perhaps the company will get into trouble if the owner cheats the IRS."

> "The owner has told us numerous times that the company can't afford to make pay raises, yet look at how much cash he is taking from the company."

As Finders, we do not want a negative perception to become a reality. We want to set the right example and be the leaders that people can look up to and respect at all times.

Employee Theft and Fraud Insurance

A company should consider purchasing employee theft and fraud insurance. This is one area that should be reviewed and possibly increased at the annual renewal of the insurance each year.

The next chapter explains some of the proactive things a Finder might consider to stop employee theft.

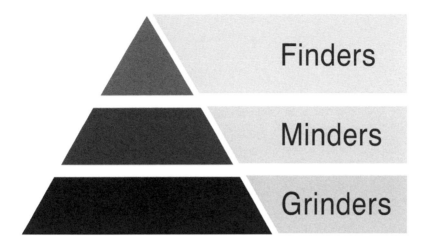

CHAPTER 8

Who's Watching the Minders?

Much of the theft that we see is done by the company's Minders, like the controller or accounting manager. (These people are sometimes called finance managers or bookkeepers.)

There is a second serious problem with Minders regarding theft from other company employees. Minders are usually not trained to catch fraud perpetrated by their coworkers. They simply do not have the experience, expertise or training to detect sophisticated fraud committed by other employees.

Who's watching your Minders?

On-Site Visits by Outsiders?

Does your company have an outside professional regularly working at your place of business each month (perhaps unannounced) to look over the accounting records and computer systems and observe the trends on financial statements or systems?

Can my CPA firm catch an embezzlement?

Business owners often ask B2B CFO® if their CPA or CPA firm can perform the function of looking over the shoulders of the controller and staff. This is a legitimate question.

CPA firms can be hired to perform fraud examinations. This is a specific engagement that will last for a limited period of time.

CPA firms are usually hired to perform tax returns and attest-function examinations. **They should not be relied upon for fraud detection when they perform any of these engagements, unless the engagement letter specifically spells out the terms (and time period) of the fraud detection.**

It's not fair to the business owner or the CPA firm to expect fraud detection unless the scope of work is so defined in the CPAs engagement letter. Please read the engagement letter from your CPA very carefully. Most attest-function examination engagement letters will say, **"Our engagement cannot be relied upon to disclose errors, illegal acts, fraud or any theft that may exist in your company."**

There is nothing wrong with your CPA making this type of statement. You need to be aware that the scope of the CPAs work may not have the verbiage to uncover any fraud or theft in your company.

> **B2B Adage**: *Do not rely upon your CPA firm to detect theft or fraud, unless you specifically engage them for this function for a specified period of time.*

Most CPA firms need to keep some distance from creating the internal controls of their clients. This is called "independence" and is an important function of our society. Otherwise, they might be viewed by the public as "auditing themselves."

Arthur Andersen's trouble with Enron is an example. Apparently, Arthur Andersen & Co. was paid more money to perform "consulting" services than it was being paid for "examination" services. The perception in the business community was that Andersen's auditors were closing their eyes to certain types of questionable business activities that should have been disclosed to the board of directors and stockholders.

From January 2nd to April 15th

The key partners of CPA firms are usually not available to the business owner between January 2nd and April 15th. The partners of CPA firms have intentionally created a business model that causes them to be too busy to leave their offices to spend quality time with a client during the busy season. This statement also holds true for most of the calendar year.

To compensate for the lack of partner time, these firms sometimes send out inexperienced staff people to perform consulting services. By "inexperienced," I mean they do not have a background working within a privately held company and are not senior level executives with 20+ years of experience.

Fraud and Experience

It is risky to assume that just because professionals have a CPA certificate, they are experienced and savvy enough to catch fraud. Most CPA firms that do income tax preparation and audit work have spent their entire careers as staff in an accounting firm. They typically have not worked full-time as a senior level executive inside a privately held company. They may not have the training or experience to detect sophisticated fraud in a company.

Basic accounting is a very small part of fraud detection. An accounting degree and a license do not always mean a CPA or the firm's staff are qualified to understand the complexities of someone trying to steal from a company. One must have years of training and experience for fraud detection.

Senior level Executives

Business owners need a seasoned senior level executive to look over the shoulders of Minders. Often, there is little separation in companies between accounting departments and operations. In these cases, the senior level executive should have experience in both accounting and operations.

We recommend that you engage this person to come to your place of business at least monthly. Allow them to look into the computer systems and at the details of the financial statements. Let them walk around to see what is happening within the company.

Meet regularly with this person to receive input as to what is happening with your business. Let your Minders be trained by this person. Let your accounting and other staff know that a seasoned professional is looking over their shoulders. This should help reduce your staff's temptation to steal.

Additionally, the senior level executive should be expected to help the company develop internal control systems and segregation of duties.

A second opinion from your CPA

After doing the above, have your CPA firm take another look at the financial statements for the company in an "independent" function.

Create a situation where your CPA firm and your senior level executives are on your team to advise you and give you input from a variety of different perspectives. This teamwork between the two different levels of disciplines should help you with the company's goals to decrease employee theft.

No professional can (or should) promise a complete elimination of fraud. There are ways, however, to prepare a strategy to help reduce or minimize fraud in a company.

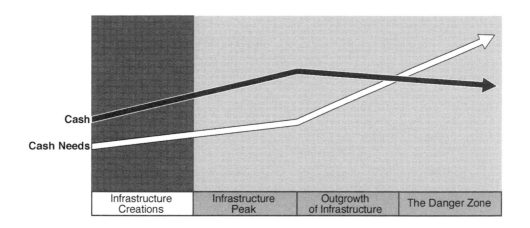

CHAPTER 9

Infrastructure Creation

You have been creating your company's infrastructure since the day you started your business. Even if you may not have been doing this intentionally, you have made the effort, regardless of your intentions.

What is infrastructure?

The word infrastructure is relatively new to our business vocabulary. The history and business definitions are:

> "The basic, underlying framework or features of a system or organization." [21]

Your Business Infrastructure

Most Finders do not methodically create a plan to build the infrastructure of the company. Rather, they typically take a Band-Aid® approach, creating their infrastructure out of necessity, and not from the perspective of long-term strategic planning. A short list of the company's infrastructure might include some of the following:

1. Intranet
2. Employees
3. Vendors
4. Computer hardware
5. Computer software
6. Outside contractors
7. Bankers
8. Lenders or leasing companies
9. Outside accountants and attorneys
10. Operating procedures and processes
11. IT staff
12. Machinery and equipment
13. Office space or buildings
14. Websites
15. Telephone systems

In the beginning, the infrastructures that Finders create are usually oriented around customer activities. The activities typically involve:

1. Finding customers
2. Closing the sale
3. Delivering goods or services
4. Invoicing
5. Collecting cash

I sometimes refer to this period as the "dating" period. Life is good. The Finder is totally focused on the customer. Tremendous efforts are made to find customers, listen to their needs, solve their problems and deliver the goods or services on time.

> **B2B Adage:** *Most Finders do not spend a lot of time methodically planning their business infrastructure.*

Short Cash Cycles

The cash cycle is typically short in this period. It is easy to get the invoice to the proper people and to have a quick turnaround on the collection of money. Overhead is typically low in the company and, while cash is tight, the Finder has a gut feeling that "this will work" and that there will always be more cash than expenses. Any excess cash allows the Finder to invest in more infrastructure. The Finder invests in people, machines, and equipment that will allow the company to make even more sales than before.

Time with the Customer

The Finder spends time with the customer and develops a relationship with the customer's key people. The Finder has a lot of energy in this period and spends much "creative time" meeting the needs of the customer in a manner that sets the Finder apart from the competition. There are few administrative distractions during this period that might take the Finder away from the focus of the customer.

Information System Infrastructure

"A well-designed information system rests on a coherent foundation that supports modifications as new business or administrative initiatives arise. Known as the information system infrastructure, the foundation consists of core telecommunications networks, databases, software, hardware, and procedures. Managed by various specialists, information systems frequently incorporate the use of general information and telecommunication utilities, such as the Internet. Owing to business globalization, an organization's infrastructure often crosses many national boundaries. Creating and maintaining such a complex infrastructure requires extensive planning and consistent implementation to handle strategic corporate initiatives." [22]

The infrastructure changes and impacts everyone who is involved as your company continues to grow.

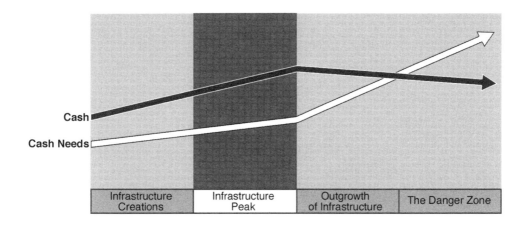

| Infrastructure Creations | Infrastructure Peak | Outgrowth of Infrastructure | The Danger Zone |

CHAPTER 10

Infrastructure Peak

The Honeymoon Phase

If you take a close look at the graph above, you will see an unusually high gap between the company's cash and cash needs. I call this the honeymoon phase, or the "infrastructure peak."

Another economic term for this period might be the ROI (Return on Investment). This period is the effect of a significant focus by the Finder during Infrastructure Creation.

The reason I refer to this cycle as the "honeymoon" period is because it gives a false sense of security about the company. The company has not yet experienced significant cash shortages. There has been such a focus on the vision of the company and the customer that an economic aberration has occurred. The aberration involves the following:

1. High customer service
2. Short cash collection cycles
3. Few customer complaints
4. Low overhead
5. Personal financial sacrifice by the Finder

Running Lean and Mean

In other words, the company has been running lean, *perhaps too lean*. The Finder and the employees have been running a 100-yard dash for about 100 miles. The excess cash gives pause to the Finder and the company employees and begins a thought process that might sound something like:

"Perhaps I should have a pay raise."

"We need to hire more people so we can take time off."

"I bet our customers would like to see us in a more impressive building."

"Do we need to give out 401(k) and health plans?"

"My spouse wants me to build a new house."

"I really need a newer vehicle."

"Can we all go on a vacation to Hawaii?"

"We need more equipment to make better products."

"Should we diversify and find other lines of business?"

The above (and similar) sentiments show the change in business attitudes during this phase. "Lean and mean" is no longer the mantra of the company. **Less thought is given to the needs of the customer during this period of time.**

More thought and energy are devoted to building "the company." The Finder starts to get pulled into directions that are unfamiliar by a host of professionals and other people who claim to know more than the business owner about how to use the company's cash. Plans and methods are created to have cash leave the company.

> **B2B Adage:** *Far too often, company resources are spent in buying things that do not always lead to excellent customer service.*

Customers Who Get in the Way?

I remember a conversation while I was at a client's office. The executives of the company were lamenting the time it took to serve their customers.

One executive exclaimed that he could get much more done if the customer would simply, "not get in the way." I looked with incredulity at this seemingly intelligent person. It was not the right time to express my feelings, but I wanted to say, "Don't you understand that the customer is the one paying your paycheck?" The attitude of these senior level executives was unbelievable, but is not uncommon for certain people within a company to lose track of trying to fill the needs of the customer.

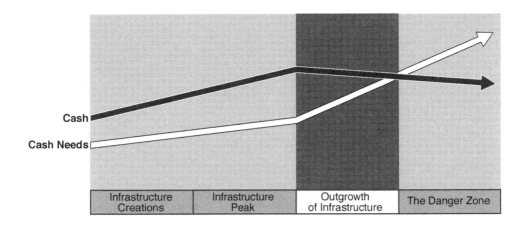

Cash			
Cash Needs			
Infrastructure Creations	Infrastructure Peak	Outgrowth of Infrastructure	The Danger Zone

CHAPTER 11
Outgrowth of Infrastructure

The Foundation Has Cracked

Let's imagine your company's building. It has a good foundation. Because of land limitations, the only way you can expand your building is by adding floors. The company's sales are growing rapidly. You need more space to deliver the additional sales, so you decide to add an additional floor to the existing building.

The expansion is a success until your company leaps in sales. The company needs more space, so a decision is made to add yet another floor to the building. However, before the new floor is completed, your contractor notifies you that the building's foundation has started to crack. You are advised to stop construction. Not only have you wasted money on the new floor, but you now are concerned that you might not be able to take care of the increased customer sales that are presently on the books. The above is an analogy for growth in most companies. From the first day of opening the company, the Finder is building a foundation, which we refer to as "infrastructure." As we discussed earlier, this foundation, or infrastructure, is made up of the company's employees, vendors, computer hardware and software, bankers, lenders, outside professionals, operating procedures, IT staff, office space, buildings, equipment, websites, telephone systems, intranets and so forth.

Infrastructure Outgrowth

Companies that experience significant growth, both in sales and the volume of transactions, typically outgrow their infrastructure.

The business reason for the outgrowth is simple: The Finder has been so busy bringing in sales that attention has not been given to the foundation (infrastructure) of the company.

The volume of sales, transactions, and employees has a collective "weight." The company's infrastructure foundation has major "cracks" and cannot support the stress of the weight. Thus, the company experiences infrastructure outgrowth. The company must now stop its normal process of sales and delivery to strengthen the foundation—otherwise, the entire company is in jeopardy.

Symptoms of the Infrastructure Outgrowth

Before we discuss the causes of this problem, let's discuss some of the *symptoms* of the problem. The symptoms of infrastructure outgrowth are easy to spot. They are typically exposed in the following areas:

Customers

1. Customer complaints increase
2. Customers begin disputing charges on invoices or statements
3. Customers refuse to accept certain goods or services
4. Orders from certain customers unexpectedly decrease
5. More time is spent on problems with smaller customers than on larger or more profitable customers

Productivity

1. Quality of goods or services decreases
2. Accounting starts giving out inaccurate information
3. The Finder needs to attend more meetings
4. Finders and Minders have longer "non-productive" work weeks
5. Equipment downtime occurs more frequently
6. Information from accounting is delayed

Employees

1. Overtime increases
2. Workforce turnover is higher
3. Employee theft of money, time, inventory, and customer lists increases
4. Employee benefit costs, such as COBRA, profit sharing, 401(k) plans
5. Quality of new hires decreases

Cash and Company Assets

1. There are periodic shortages of cash
2. Average days a receivable is collectible increases
3. Inventory that is not sellable increases
4. The owner or owners start personally lending money to the company to cover cash needs

Software, Websites, Computer Hardware

1. Computer crashes occur more frequently
2. Viruses or other software problems arise
3. The telephone or voice mail systems become inadequate or very expensive to operate
4. The IT department unexpectedly requests computer hardware or software purchases
5. Website problems take longer to fix
6. Bids to convert to new software products are higher than expected
7. The owner feels there is a never-ending black hole of money spent on computers and systems, with no ending black hole.

Vendors

1. Vendors begin delaying delivery to the company
2. Vendors are not paid on time and become disillusioned
3. Valuable time is spent finding suitable vendors

Overhead

1. Overhead unexpectedly increases
2. Legal, accounting, and other professional fees increase
3. Insurance costs increase
4. Company receives fines and notices from the IRS or other governmental agencies

5. Health insurance rates significantly increase

Lending and Borrowing

1. The cost of borrowing money increases
2. Company is unable to borrow enough money from banks or lenders
3. Company receives unexpected requests for documents from banks or lenders
4. Banker complaints about the accuracy of internal accounting documents increase
5. Banker complaints about the delay of accounting information increase
6. The Finder perceives that bankers or lenders are backing away from the company

This list could be much longer, but you get the idea. The company is not firing on all cylinders and the problems seem to compound daily.

Planning for a Growth Company

Finders, by definition, are visionaries, dreamers, idea generators, innovators, motivators and catalysts for change. Do you notice something missing from this list? How about the word "planners?"

Finders loathe detailed planning of infrastructure. It is boring to them. They do not like the tedious work. They typically are not skilled in the subjects related to the infrastructure of their company. Finders get frustrated spending time listening to "geeks" or other professionals who not only cost a lot of money but seem to be self-serving. They do not see the benefit of spending hours, days, weeks or months in detailed planning of infrastructure. To a Finder, this planning time takes away from finding customers and building the company's future vision.

> **B2B Adage:** *The failure to plan infrastructure will eventually hurt the company and will take away from finding customers at some point in the future.*

Planning Comments from Others

Gardner H. Russell, Napoleon Hill and W. Clement Stone have commented on the importance of goals and planning:

> "In the absence of clearly defined goals, we are forced to concentrate on activity and ultimately become enslaved by it." [23]

> "To succeed in anything, it is necessary to know the rules and understand how to apply them. It is necessary to study, to learn, to think, and to plan." [24]

Work the Weakness

As a Finder, there is nothing wrong with admitting that you do not like detailed planning of infrastructure. Delegate this process if you do not like it and/or if it takes too much of your time. It is your responsibility, however, to make sure it gets done.

The Future of Your Company

Please take a few minutes to fill in the blanks next to the following questions:

Estimate your company's gross sales:

This year: $_____
Five years from now: $_____
Ten years from now: $_____

Name the company's three most dangerous competitors:

1.   _____
2.   _____
3.   _____

Now you are ready to answer three key questions. The answers to these questions may take some time for you to complete. Be as detailed as you can and write down the answers to these questions.

1. What are your most dangerous competitors actively planning to take away your current customers?

2. What do you need to do to keep ahead of your most dangerous competitors who will be actively trying to keep you from achieving your future sales goals?

3. Who is going to be on your team to build your infrastructure to help achieve the level of sales you want many years from today and to help keep your company from being killed by your most dangerous competition?

Share This Information

You might consider sharing the above information with your team. If you do not have the right team players, go get them. It is better to get them on board with your company than to possibly have them hired by your competitors.

Share the sales goals that you want to achieve five and ten years from now, plus the other information you documented from this exercise.

Assign your team to arrive at a budget to build the infrastructure needed to support your goals.

The Job as a Finder

In short, your job as a Finder is as follows:

1. Set future sales and growth goals.
2. Hire the right people to build the company's infrastructure.
3. Give the right people the money to achieve your infrastructure.
4. Make sure your infrastructure team does as assigned. Fire them if they fail and replace them with better people.
5. Go find customers, open new markets, dream and have some fun.

> **B2B Adage**: *Your competitors are actively planning today to take away your customers tomorrow.*

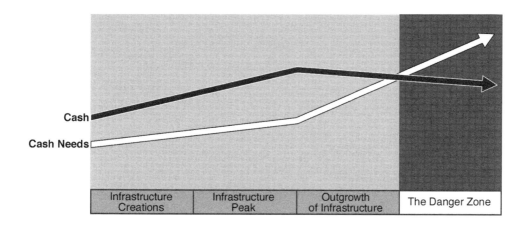

CHAPTER 12

The Danger Zone

The above graph shows that the cash needs of the company exceed available cash. This is **The Danger Zone**. The future of the company may be in jeopardy.

There are dozens of reasons why the cash needs exceed the available cash. Some of those reasons are outlined in the preceding chapter, which deal with the outgrowth of the company's infrastructure.

Regardless of the reasons, the company is either in serious trouble or is headed in the wrong direction.

> **B2B Adage**: *The Danger Zone is created when the cash needs of a company far exceed the cash available to meet those needs.*

Albert Einstein

Dr. Stephen R. Covey wrote the following observation that is credited to Albert Einstein:

> "The significant problems we face cannot be solved at the same level of thinking we were at when we created them." [25]

Finders need to think differently than they did before they hit **The Danger Zone** which by definition, is a significant problem. Certain Finders may have never faced such challenges in their careers, which is one of the reasons the Small Business Administration (SBA) has published that 30% of new businesses fail during the first two years of being open, 50% during the first five years and 66% during the first ten years.[26]

Managing the Finding Time

The inception of a company is a romantic time for Finders. Yes, there are cash flow and other business problems, but the enjoyment the Finder has in the Finding activities seems to outweigh other issues.

Sometimes, for the first time in their lives, the Finders are actually getting to do what they want to do for a living. Some are golfing with key people; some are thinking and dreaming; some are spending time with intelligent associates working on the details of the dream.

Before the business honeymoon is over, the romantic Finding activities give a joyful sense of fulfillment to Finders. They can put up with pain from others as long as they can spend the majority of their time in Finding activities. The future looks bright to the Finder, even if there is little or no cash in the company.

The business honeymoon is over when the Finder stops spending most of their time in Finding activities. Seemingly overnight, the Finder is spending most of his or her time doing administrative and other non-Finding activities.

> **B2B Adage:** *We have yet to see a Finder with the desire or goal to start a business to spend time on accounting and computer problems, yet far too many spend too much time resolving those things.*

What went wrong after the business honeymoon? Well, the weight of the infrastructure caused the Finder's time to shift to non-Finding activities.

Instead of spending time on things that used to be fun, Finders are now spending valuable time doing things they despise and never imagined they would do before they started the business.

The Finder's Time Shift

The trend slowly moves from being a Finder towards becoming a Minder or a Grinder.

The Finder's time shift is predictable during these transitional phases. The following information should not be viewed in terms of absolutes, but as an observation of trends, based upon decades of experience watching Finders become Minders and/or Grinders during *The Danger Zone*:

Activity	Infrastructure Growth	Infrastructure Peak	Outgrowth of Infrastructure	The Danger Zone
Finding	85%	80%	70%	30%
Minding	5%	15%	25%	60%
Grinding	10%	5%	5%	10%
	100%	100%	100%	100%

A graph of the shift to Minding time would look something like the following. (The remaining time percentage is often spent in Grinding activities.)

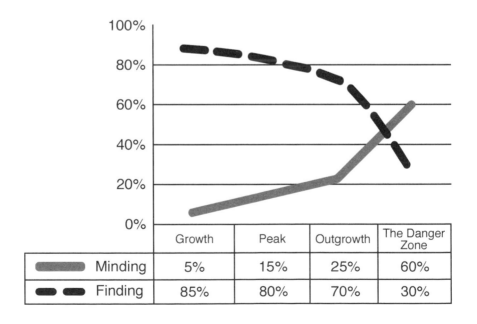

	Growth	Peak	Outgrowth	The Danger Zone
Minding	5%	15%	25%	60%
Finding	85%	80%	70%	30%

Activities during the Time Shift

In previous chapters we documented that a Finder's principle goal is to build relationships that cause the company to grow. We identified a few things that Finders do during the Infrastructure Creation period of the company, such as:

1. Building relationships with customers
2. Creating relationships with vendors
3. Delegating tasks to employees or associates
4. Causing sales and cash to come into the company

During the time shift from Finding to Minding, we see that the Finder spends less time in the above activities. The shift is now to Minding activities, such as the following:

1. Managing the company's cash
2. Lengthy meetings with accounting and administrative staff
3. Many meetings with bankers and lenders
4. Meetings with attorneys and accountants
5. Spending significant time deciding which checks will be written
6. Purchasing and installing computer systems
7. Installing computer software
8. Entering transactions into the computer
9. Firing staff
10. Hiring new staff (who typically are not trained properly)
11. Taking deposits to the bank
12. Managing check payments

A person might ask, "What is wrong with these activities?" Good question, which is easily answered.

- Finders are not skilled and/or do not have the passion to perform the above tasks. Additionally, they do not have patience or time to properly train or to perform these tasks.

- All of the above take the Finder away from Finding activities, which often has serious consequences.

- No business owner starts a business with the goal of doing the above activities. They typically loathe the very thought of performing these tasks.

Consequences of the Time Shift

During **The Danger Zone**, the Finder is dealing with infrastructure "weight" that distracts and then eventually destroys. The distraction may come in several forms, such as:

1. Loss of current customers
2. Damaged business relationships due to the Finder's stress
3. Death of the Finder's dream
4. Loss of Finder's enthusiasm or energy
5. Divorce
6. Damaged relationships with children and family members
7. Diminished health of the Finder
8. Loss of future customers
9. Death of the company

The distraction items above do not include all the damage to employees, families of employees, vendors and other important relationships of the Finder.

Why Does a Finder Become a Minder?

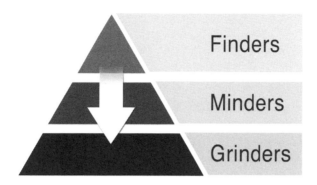

Why do you think that Finders stop doing what they love to do, which are Finding activities, and start doing what they hate to do, which are Minding activities?

The answer to the question is very simple. However, the discipline needed to find the solution to the problem may be complex. Most likely, the Finder will need outside help during *The Danger Zone*.

I Will Fix the Problem

Most Finders are Type A personalities. Many were in athletics when they were younger. Many excelled academically, in music or other disciplines and are very competitive. They have now started a business and have helped the company grow from the sheer efforts of their intellect, personalities and skills. Problems, some of them of a serious nature, have arisen in the past. When those problems arose, the Finder jumped in with both feet and solved them. There might have been some personal satisfaction in quickly solving problems.

The Changes Are Not So Easy This Time

The infrastructure problems of the company are not so easily fixed today. The company is now too large for a quick fix. There is too much weight from infrastructure problems with customers, vendors, employees, subcontractors, computers, software, litigation, bankers, governmental agencies, cash shortages and so forth. More knowledge is needed to fix the infrastructure than presently exists within the company. Albert Einstein's observation now haunts the Finder:

> "The significant problems we face cannot be solved at the same level of thinking we were at when we created them." [27]

Someone to Trust

Finders often do not delegate certain tasks to people simply because they do not trust others within the company. In this situation, we need to ask:

1. Is the problem with the Finder?
2. Is the problem with the Minder or Grinder?

The solution to the dilemma may be a difficult one to find if the Finder is the reason for the lack of trust. Sometimes the lack of trust is because the company does not have written policies and procedures (infrastructure) that give comfort to the Finder that the job will be done correctly. Often, the Finder feels that nobody can do the job correctly. Sometimes the Finder simply has an issue with trust. If this is the case, it may be good for the Finder to find a confidant to whom he can talk about this trust issue. Ultimately, the Finder must delegate tasks in order to grow the company to avoid or to escape *The Danger Zone*.

B2B Adage*:* *The Finder must learn to trust people. Employees should be terminated from the company if they are not trustworthy.*

Sometimes the trust issue stems from prior actions of the Minder or Grinder. If the lack of trust is because the Minder or Grinder has stolen or cheated the company, the next step is very simple: Fire them—even if they are family members. The Finder wants such a person working elsewhere. It is a rare situation in which the Finder will be able to rehabilitate dishonest employees. If the Finder has dishonest employees, even family members, the Finder has only one course of action, and that is to terminate the relationship and hire someone who is trustworthy.

B2B Adage: *Good management is defined as the accomplishment of the goals and objectives of the company through the actions of other people.*

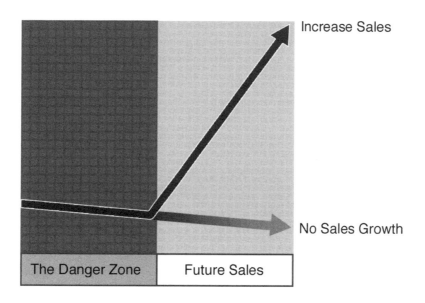

CHAPTER 13

Escaping the Danger Zone

Ideally, owners of privately held businesses will read this book and apply its principles before their company hits **The Danger Zone**.

Some business owners may be in this condition before they pick up this book. We need to now address how to get out of **The Danger Zone**.

Future Sales with the Right Margins

One of two things will happen with a company that enters **The Danger Zone**: sales will increase or decrease. *Sales and net profit rarely stay flat*. A Finder who will leave Minding enough to increase sales (with good profit margins) might have some likelihood of escaping **The Danger Zone**.

Cash or Sales?

Which came first: The chicken or the egg? Which comes first in **The Danger Zone**: sales or cash? The answer to this question for the Finder is obvious. The Finder will need to find sales and other people in the company need to find cash. This is where the discussion in earlier chapters of this book about surrounding yourself with senior level executives is very important.

> **B2B Adage***:*   *During **The Danger Zone,** the Finder hires sales people and senior level executives to help the company find cash.*

The Danger Zone Results

The options for a Finder of a company that enters **The Danger Zone** are limited. A few of the options are:

1. Changes habits and grows sales, which increases cash

2. Borrows money

3. Sells valuable company or personal assets to put cash into the company

4. Escalates the Minding activities, which causes sales to decrease, which has the likelihood of a bad exit strategy for the company

> **B2B Adage***:*   *Leaders make tough decisions. There is no benefit in shuffling chairs on the deck of the Titanic. Leaders look to the future and avoid the icebergs that are in the path of their company.*

The Shift from Minding to Finding

Ultimately, the Finder must leave Minding to others to escape *The Danger Zone*. This shift requires discipline and, possibly, money. There is no choice in the matter. The Finder must find someone who can watch over the Minding activities of the company.

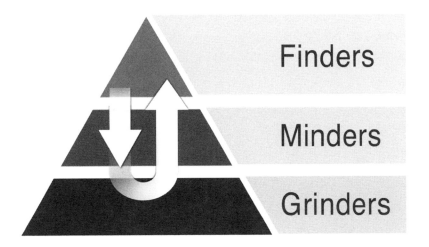

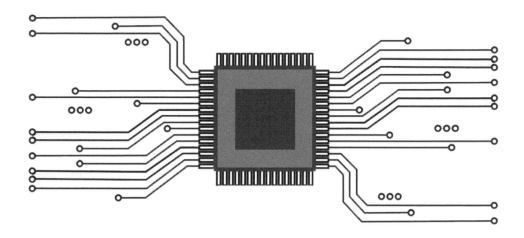

CHAPTER 14

Moore's Law and the Finder

Laws impact our daily lives, regardless of whether we are consciously aware of it. For example, the law of gravity is real. Some could argue that gravity does not exist, but they would change their minds the next time something very heavy drops on their foot.

Let's discuss Moore's Law, an important law that exists within every computer system. This law is very real. One could argue that it does not exist and is not applicable to one's business. Just like arguing against the law of gravity, however, one runs the risk of failing by ignoring Moore's Law.

Moore's Law Defined

"In 1965, Gordon E. Moore—the co-founder of Intel—postulated in a magazine article that the number of transistors that can be packed into a given unit of space will double about every two years. Moore's insight became a prediction, which in turn became the golden rule known as Moore's Law." [28]

Obviously, the speed of doubling the number of transistors on a chip every two years will eventually slow down. Scientists may find a way to make computers without transistors.

Regardless, the future will bring faster computer systems. The demand for computer speed will continue in order to keep up with the need to run more sophisticated software. Complex software needs speed, so computers must keep up with the demand.

B2B Adage: *Computers in the future will be faster than computers you purchase today, which means you must have an active computer replacement plan.*

A Company's Computer Infrastructure

A Finder may ask, "Why should I be concerned about computers being faster in the future?" Below are some possible answers to this question:

- Your competitors are making plans to have better technology than you in order to take away your customers.

- To survive, you want to start budgeting money to replace your existing computer system (file servers, PCs, modems, etc.) at least every two or three years. Otherwise, you will be behind before you know what hit you.

Computer Planning

The following are tasks that may be delegated to others within the organization who can report this important information to you.

Hardware budget for the next five years:

- Year #1: $_____
- Year #2: $_____
- Year #3: $_____
- Year #4: $_____
- Year #5: $_____

Website, software, intranet and technology budget for the next five years:

- Year #1: $_____
- Year #2: $_____
- Year #3: $_____
- Year #4: $_____
- Year #5: $_____

A Lot of Courage

Planning for the future will most likely take a different level of thinking than has been used in the past. Albert Einstein is credited with saying:

> "Any intelligent fool can make things bigger and more complex... It takes a touch of genius—and a lot of courage to move in the opposite direction." [29]

Finders can't expect to be competitive unless they adopt a new way of thinking about the company's future technology. An identification of money to be spent on future technology must be documented and communicated to key employees, bankers, and trusted advisors.

This new way of thinking about spending on technology is difficult for some Finders. Some do not trust this way of thinking and feel money would be better spent on other things.

Write down the amount of money you feel your most powerful competitors are going to spend on technology in the future. Now, exceed that amount.

Technology Is the Future

Regardless of the industry, the future belongs to those dedicated to technology. Moore's Law favors the disciplined Finder who uses this law to take the company to new levels.

Conversely, Finders who avoid Moore's Law and fail to budget for technology expenses will be punished by the market and by the competition.

B2B Adage: *A company that does not comply with Moore's Law (i.e., investing in technology and computer infrastructure, regardless of the industry) will be severely punished by this law.*

CHAPTER 15

Bankers and Lenders:
Friends or Foes?

Finders sometimes have a love-hate relationship with bankers. They love bankers when they receive enough money (at the right price and terms) and hate them when they don't.

Finders often spend too much time Minding their bankers and lenders. They will spend many hours trying to find the right bank to get the company the right amount of money.

Bankers and lenders are critical to our economic society. Without them, our economy would come to a screeching halt.

Bankers are not perfect. Just like people in any industry, there are good bankers and bad bankers. Some bankers are the best their profession has to offer and others are an embarrassment to the banking and lending profession. The goal is to find the good ones and build long-term relationships with them for the future success of you and your company.

Increased Sales vs. Increased Cash Flow

Bankers want to know that your company is going in the right direction and has the tools to succeed. Finders often get very frustrated with a banker when their company's sales are going through the roof and the banker will not lend them more money. A banker understands that a significant increase in sales will not necessarily mean an increase in cash flow. In fact, the opposite often happens.

> **B2B Adage:** *A significant increase in sales some-times means that the company might have a decrease in cash, which is the opposite of what Finders expect with sales increases.*

The reason a growth company has less cash is because the cash is tied up in accounts receivable, payroll, inventory, fixed assets and other such items.

The Bank – Your Customer?

A good way to look at a bank is to try to pretend it is your customer What do you do for your customers?

You try to find out what they want so they will pay you money for your goods or services. You may spend weeks, months, or even years trying to determine your customer's needs so they will pay you.

Bankers can be viewed the same way. What do they want and what do you have to do to legally get their money?

Bankers want customers who:

1. Issue accurate interim financial statements on a timely basis
2. File timely tax returns prepared by a reputable CPA
3. Have an owner who understands their financial statements
4. Invest in computer systems and talent to help with internal controls
5. Hire senior level executives to help the Finder avoid Minding and Grinding activities
6. Have acceptable key ratios (Key Performance Indicators)
7. Are going in the right direction

Naturally, you do not want to give too much away to the bank. Personal guarantees and other such items may have serious ramifications for both you and your company. Find out what the bank needs and plan a strategy with your senior level advisors on how to obtain loans at the best possible price.

Join their Game

I have been in countless meetings where bankers have started to explain key ratios of a Finder's company only to see the Finder become disinterested and/or bored. Finders often do not understand why bankers look at "old" data, such as the information on a balance sheet, to judge whether or not their company should receive a loan. Finders do not always understand why bankers do not take into account the Finder's enthusiasm about the company's future growth and other opportunities.

You are not playing the game the right way if you show frustration to the bank. In a sports analogy, you are letting the referees control the game. You should consider setting aside your feelings and beat the banker at their own game.

So, how is this done? How does a Finder beat the bank at its own game? The answers lie within the very nature of you as a Finder:

1. Take control
2. Understand
3. Lead
4. Sell

There's no reason for an owner to be ill-prepared for the meeting with the banker. Have information prepared in advance to discuss with them. By information, I do not mean the typical information that Finders want to give bankers, such as projections, promises and estimates of the future. By information I mean:

1. Correct and timely financial statements
2. Calculations of key ratios
3. Interpretations of key ratios
4. Simple projections with a list of assumptions
5. KPIs (Key Performance Indicators) specific to your company's industry and sales volume

Key Ratios

Below are some key ratios and information you should consider documenting in preparation for the meeting with your banker (this list will vary by industry):

1. Working capital
2. Current ratio
3. Quick ratio
4. Debt-to-equity ratio
5. Days in accounts receivable
6. Gross profit margin
7. Inventory turnover ratio

What If I Have a Bad Current Ratio?

As a Finder, you can't afford not to know your working capital and your current ratio. That ratio should be close to the industry ratio found by comparing the company to the KPIs by SIC Code and similar sales volume. Often the working capital and current ratios are not where they should be to fulfill the cash flow needs of the company and to meet banking requirements. To avoid this pitfall, here are some strategies:

1. Plan ways to take current debt to long-term debt.

2. Look at possible ways to move related-party transactions into owners' equity.

3. Ask your banker for advice on this subject. Your banker will be impressed that you understand this topic and will most likely be eager to help you solve this problem.

Key ratios are best used if you have a two or three-year historical analysis with your current numbers.

EBITDA

EBITDA is an acronym for earnings before interest, tax, depreciation and amortization. It is a measure of a company's operating performance.

Bankers will want to know your company's EBITDA, which can be calculated if the company has timely and accurate financial information. Bo Birlingham wrote:

> "Think of it (EBITDA) as the amount of cash a company generates in a year after paying all of its operating costs and expenses before covering what it owes in taxes and interest and before deducting depreciation and amortization. It is thus a better reflection of the business's operating condition than, say, net earnings." [30]

There are several reasons your banker might want to know a company's correct EBITDA:

1. **Debt Service** – Does the company have the future cash flow to service the principal payments on all notes payable, including any new possible notes in progress?

2. **Distributions** – Assuming the company is a pass-through entity, does the company have enough cash flow to fund distributions to owners to pay for federal, state and local income taxes from the profits of the company?

3. **Unexpected Events** – Does the company have enough cash flow to fund any unexpected events or expenses in the future?

There might be reasons the business owner may want to know the company's EBITDA. For example, they might want to have an understanding of the company's possible value. Frederick D. Lipman is quoted in our proprietary book, *The Exit Strategy Handbook:*

> "A number of businesses are valued by buyers based upon accounting earnings or income. Indeed, one of the most common methods of valuation is the so-called EBITDA method. This involves the determination of your accounting earnings before interest, taxes, depreciation, and amortization (EBITDA), and multiplication of the EBITDA by the relevant multiplier to obtain a business valuation." [31]

An Interesting Success Story

Bankers and business owners can work together to create a business situation where both parties win. With some help from our firm, the following story started out as a lose-lose situation but turned into a win-win situation. (The names in this story have been changed.)

I received an urgent call from two owners of a privately held company, Jacob and Richard. They had received very positive reviews about my firm from a bank. They had an "emergency" and we arranged for a meeting early the next day.

Jacob and Richard shared the same office. They were 50-50% owners of a company that employed about 300 people. They were pleasant to visit with but under much stress.

The reason for the emergency was that their bank, Alberta Western Bank, notified them that their multi-million-dollar working capital line of credit would be revoked in exactly 60 days. They explained to me that the revocation of the line of credit would mean bankruptcy. The intent of the meeting was to have my firm, which has wonderful relationships with important banks, introduce them to another bank that might give them a line of credit so they could continue their operations.

I asked Jacob and Richard why the bank wanted to revoke the company's line of credit in 60 days. Their answer was interesting. The bank was concerned with their lack of timeliness and accuracy of the company's financial statements. They told me the bank had not seen financial information about their company for nearly a year. They did not know why the bank felt the financial statements were incorrect.

This was an opportunity to teach these two dynamic owners about bankers and how to deal with them. First, I explained that there was no reason to go to a different bank. No bank that works with my firm would consider lending money to a company that had not submitted financial information for eleven and a half months. No bank would consider lending money if the financial information was materially wrong. I explained that they didn't need another bank, but they needed to quickly get information to their current bank and ask for an extension on their line of credit.

This was not the response that Jacob and Richard expected and their stress level visibly increased. It was time for them to give me more information.

I asked, "Who is responsible for giving the financial information to Alberta Western Bank?" Dean, their controller, had that responsibility. We talked for a few minutes about Dean. He had been the company's controller for a few years and was paid an annual salary of about $150,000. They both liked Dean but didn't know why he was submitting financial information to the bank that was almost a year late and inaccurate. I asked if Dean could chat with us about this emergency and explain the issues the bank had with the company's financial information.

Dean was a tenured accountant and had good communication skills. I politely asked him if he knew about the situation with the bank and the ramifications to him if the company went out of business during the next few months. He was very aware of the situation and the ramifications of the possible revocation of the company's line of credit. When asked why the financial information was eleven and a half months late and incorrect, his reply was that the two owners, Jacob and Richard, had given him other higher priority responsibilities.

I then looked at Jacob and Richard, who were shocked to hear this information from Dean. Jacob turned to me and asked if I could "solve the problem." We spent about thirty minutes to create a possible solution. I left their office and started working with Dean.

Dean explained that basic information, such as invoices to customers, invoices from vendors, checks and payroll had not been put into the company's computer system for almost a year. The company did not have the staff to input this backlog into the computer system. Additionally, the bank's sixty-day revocation letter gave the company no time to look at résumés on job boards to hire people to help with this emergency.

My recommendation, which was followed, was to call a placement company. They made a call and two people were found within a few hours. They could work seven days a week at the company's office.

Both of them scored highly on their proficiency with the company's software. They were both at my client's office at 8:00 a.m. the next morning to begin the data entry tasks.

Jacob, Richard and I quickly met with the bank. We made sure the bank was updated several times a week about the progress. The necessary work to produce a timely and accurate financial statement was completed in about fifty days. Much to the surprise of the bank and Jacob and Richard, the updated financial information showed that the company was doing very well, both in profits and in the key ratios (bank loan covenants).

Fred, the key banker at Alberta Western Bank didn't have much time to discuss the financial information and to renegotiate the line of credit. He invited us to meet at a Phoenix Suns basketball game. The bank owned prime seats and the game was very entertaining. We met at a VIP lounge during halftime and hammered out a win-win arrangement regarding my client's request for a loan extension. That extension was granted by the bank's loan committee before the sixty-day deadline.

My firm provided another very pleasant but unexpected service to Jacob and Richard. I got to know them well during the 55 plus days it took to renew the line of credit. They both asked me about their personal FICO credit scores, with the desire to make them much higher. Their low FICO scores were stopping them from being able to purchase personal assets, such as homes for their families.

The reason their FICO scores were so low was because they had each purchased dozens of vehicles and equipment with personal loan guarantees. The individual loans for these assets were shown on their individual personal credit and caused their FICO scores to decrease.

These assets were used exclusively by the company they owned. The company made monthly payments on these notes. I asked permission to meet with Fred from Alberta Western Bank. A win-win plan was presented to Fred. Alberta Western Bank subsequently offered a multi-million-dollar note to purchase the dozens of individual notes related to these assets. The new note had great terms and the monthly principal payment was significantly lower than the combined principal payments of the dozens of notes payable that were on their personal credit.

This plan not only allowed Jacob and Richard to improve their personal FICO credit scores, but also significantly increased the company's cash flow due to the decreased principal on the new note with Alberta Western Bank. This was another win-win for both the company and the bank.

CHAPTER 16

Current and Future Different Customers

This chapter gives additional emphasis to the cost of a Finder moving into Minding and Grinding activities. This topic is so important that it warrants additional information to see what happens to customers during the "transition" of a Finder to a Minder or a Grinder. Your company's customers are its lifeblood.

As Finders, we spend a lot of time and money looking for and satisfying the business needs of our customers. We then try to deliver our goods and services with the quality and timeliness expected by the customer. We often give them terms to pay their invoices in a manner that will not upset them to the point that they would want to use one of our competitors.

Unfortunately, far too many Finders take their eyes off customers during the downward spiral to a Minder or Grinder. It's easy for Finders to get distracted. Our proprietary book, *The Exit Strategy Handbook,* quotes the founder of Crate and Barrell who wrote succinctly about this subject:

> "Getting distracted is the biggest problem entrepreneurs face." [32]

Below is another review of the graph that shows the Finder's transition to Minding through the infrastructure changes discussed in previous chapters.

Finder Migration Stages

The following is a graph presented earlier in this book with the assumption that the remaining time not shown below may be in Grinding time for the Finder.

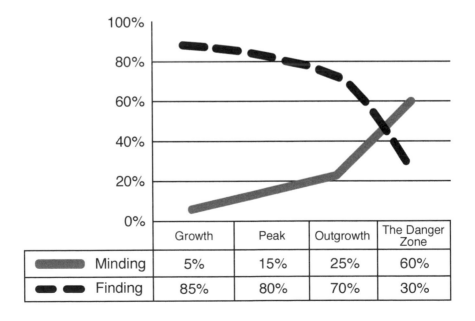

	Growth	Peak	Outgrowth	The Danger Zone
Minding	5%	15%	25%	60%
Finding	85%	80%	70%	30%

The migration of a Finder into Minding activities has a negative impact as it relates to the current customers of the company. This migration has stages that all relate to the time and energy the Finder spends in Minding activities.

Stage I – Distance
State II – Irritation
State III – Courting
Stage IV – Departure
Stage V – Sales Decrease
Stage VI – Change or Fold

Stage I - Distance

The Finder pulls back in quality and quantity time spent with their customer. Consequently, the Finder is less visible to the customer. The Finder has the intention to spend time with the customer and has periodic thoughts such as, "I'll give them a call next week." The next week passes and the weeks turn into months.

Stage II - Irritation

The customer was used to the Finder giving them time and attention. They don't understand the new lack of attention.

Consequently, the Finder becomes less important to the customer. The customer may begin to pay bills late, make short-payments on invoices, create change orders, take other actions that demonstrate dissatisfaction. The Finder, who is now more involved in Minding activities, starts to harbor resentment toward the customer. In times past, the Finder would go see the customer, maybe take them to lunch, or on a golf outing to smooth things over. Today, the Finder feels compelled to stay in the office to handle the daily crisis. The Finder may shoot the customer a terse email or may send a subordinate to the customer to solve the problem. The relationship between the customer and the Finder weakens.

Stage III - Courting

Eventually, the customer leaks to the Finder's competition that the door may be open for a preliminary discussion. The competition jumps at the chance and does everything possible to steal the customer. Sometimes the competitor fails, but, all too often, the competitor gets a foot in the door and starts a relationship with the Finder's customer. The wining and dining begin. Promises are made. Competitive proposals are presented. Meanwhile, the Finder is back at the office, buried in Minding activities and totally unaware of the competition's progress.

Stage IV - Departure

Time passes and the distance between the Finder and the customer increases. The relationship between the customer and the Finder's competition warms up. Over time, the customer simply leaves the Finder to pursue greener pastures with the Finder's competition.

Stage V - Sales Decrease

As customers leave, the Finder spends even more time Minding by managing cash and doing other day-to-day activities. Sales decrease. Cash flow becomes a problem. The company is headed in the wrong direction.

Stage VI - Change or Fold

The Finder, realizing that customers are leaving, now has a couple of choices: (1) Let the company go out of business or (2) Hire someone to mind the business while the Finder goes out to do what he or she is trained to do—bring customers to the business. The success or failure of the company will depend on the Finder's ability to bring in customers, and the new Minder's ability to hold down the fort and to find resources for the Finder's success. A good team effort may produce positive results.

The Future Different Customer

One of the dangers of Finders becoming Minders has to do with the subject of the company's future "different customers."

A "future different customer," in B2B CFO® terms, is not a new customer that will buy the goods or services that the Finder's company sells today. Rather, the future different customer is a customer that exists in the future who will possibly purchase goods and services that the Finder has not yet created.

This topic relates to you. As a Finder you have choices:

1. You can get out of Minding, begin to dream, invest in technology and begin to find new markets and engage the future different customers, or:

2. You can sit back, spend time Minding and let your competition find the future different customers that might have been yours.

The future different customers will be created and found either by you or your competition. The choice is yours and depends on the discipline you have to spend time Finding. You need the time to dream, plan, visualize, research and "pull" others into the future.

>   **B2B Adage:** *Someone is spending time with your current and future different customer. If not you, it will be your competition.*

CHAPTER 17

The Black Clouds that Haunt

Most Finders live each day with things that bother them about their businesses. They lose a lot of sleep over some of these issues and often wish they could find someone to make these problems go away. The purpose of this chapter is to identify some of those concerns which I call Black Clouds and to propose possible solutions.

Black Cloud #1 – Decision Making

Finders are by and large quick decision-makers. This is one of the attributes that sets them apart from others in our society. They quickly gather facts and use their intuition to make decisions. This is a good trait and is necessary for good leadership. This trait, however, can lead to disaster if the facts the Finder is using to make key decisions are erroneous.

Most Finders are very intelligent, regardless of their formal education. This being said, one must realize that it is highly probable that the Finders of one's competition are also very intelligent. In the long run, the goal is to make better decisions and to out-think the competition; otherwise, the Finder runs the risk of being beaten by competitors. The question then becomes, "How does a Finder make better decisions than the competition?"

Business owners can increase the probability of making a bad decision if the information they are using to make the decision is erroneous.

B2B Adage: *Bad financial information typically leads to bad decision making.*

Conversely, owners can increase their probability of making good decisions if the information they are using to make the decision is correct. One of the reasons a Finder must invest in infrastructure is to be able to receive accurate and timely information from the accounting department. Cutting corners poses too great a risk.

B2B Adage: *If you expect to beat your competition, you must have better financial information infrastructure than your competition.*

Black Cloud #2 – Control

Few things bother a Finder more than feeling a loss of control over the company. Finders who own growth companies sometimes feel as if they are steering a large ship without a rudder.

Feeling out of control typically results from failure to build a proper infrastructure. Some of the infrastructure areas that cause the most frustrations are:

1. Accounting
2. Computer hardware and software
3. Management data
4. Websites
5. Intranets
6. Backup of data

An owner should never relinquish total control of important infrastructure areas. This does not mean an owner needs to be a micro-manager of these areas. It does mean that one should hire the best people available so that one can trust what others are doing for the company.

Original Documents

An owner should never let the original version of important documents leave the company. There is no reason to ever let important documents leave the company's premises. It is an owner's right and responsibility to maintain control over original source documents. Otherwise, the owner loses a certain amount of control over the company. That loss of control may haunt the owner during future litigation, IRS audits or Department of Labor audits.

> **B2B Adage:** *A Finder should never relinquish control of the company.*

Data Backup

An owner's infrastructure processes should guarantee a backup of key data.

Every company of any value should have a well-documented "disaster recovery program" (DRP). The DRP is to be prepared for an unanticipated disaster that could cripple a company. Examples of disasters might include:

1. Fire at the corporate offices that house the company's hardware and software
2. Hacking of the company's hardware and software
3. Complete loss of control over the company's website(s) or other key data
4. Internal theft of hardware and software by employees
5. Act of God events (tornados, hurricanes, flooding, etc.)

Disaster Recover (DRP) Insurance

Owners might consider purchasing disaster recovery insurance that might pay the company cash to replace lost sales, revenue, operating expenses or the cost of moving the corporate office to a temporary location.

Black Cloud #3 - April 15th

A Finder and I were in a meeting in Scottsdale, Arizona. The Finder was a referral from a bank. We were enjoying a pleasant conversation discussing both of our companies. He was in a unique industry and was experiencing significant growth in his company.

I asked a simple question, "Do you receive accurate internal projections about the amount of money you will owe the IRS on April 15th?"

His demeanor instantly changed. "Let me ask you a question. Why did my CPA make me write a check to the IRS for $138,000 last week when my company doesn't even make any money?"

Finders often live their lives with a black cloud related to the subject of income taxes. They either have had bad experiences, such as the one mentioned above, or have heard about bad experiences from peers. They usually are expecting something bad when April 15th hits.

There is no reason for a Finder to walk around with this April 15th black cloud. Income taxes are, after all, just math calculations. Mathematical calculations can be computed at any time, assuming the information being used to make the calculations is accurate.

B2B Adage: *Many Finders spend too much energy worrying about the amount of money they will owe the IRS on April 15th.*

A Solution to April 15th

There is a solution to the April 15th problem. Below are four steps for one to follow to resolve this issue. Business owners may sleep better at night and can get rid of this black cloud if they delegate and make sure that competent people do the following:

1. Create accurate financial statements
2. Issue timely internal financial statements
3. Calculate estimated income taxes monthly
4. Have the calculations verified quarterly from the company's independent tax CPA

Accurate Financial Statements

Moore's Law, discussed earlier in this book, has significantly impacted this topic of accurate financial statements.

On the positive side, it has created opportunities for Finders to have very good computers and accounting software at a minimal cost. Before personal computers were commercially available, a business owner might need to invest six-figures in computer infrastructure for accounting hardware and software. Today, a Finder can purchase hardware and software to help run the business at a fraction of the cost that was required a few decades ago.

The bad news is that much of the accounting software that can be purchased today does not require skilled people to input financial information, such as cash disbursements, cash receipts, or bills from vendors.

A Finder's natural tendency is to invest as little cash as possible in the latest computer hardware and software. Consequently, we see people who input data into the Finder's computer systems with no idea if the information is correct. We then see the classic effect of GIGO—garbage in, garbage out. Sometimes, we discover that accounting staff have overstated their abilities when they interviewed for the job. Sometimes we determine that the accounting staff had the basic skills when the company first started but do not have the knowledge when the company is several times larger than it was when the employee was hired.

We also see the complication of related-party transactions. Finders have a tendency to create multiple wholly owned companies. The internal accounting staff typically can input data, but has no idea as to whether the data as it relates to the various entities is right or wrong.

> **B2B Adage**: *Your company must have accurate finan-cial statements in order to make accurate projections of the income taxes that will be owed on April 15th.*

It is our recommendation that the Finder's financial statements be accurate each and every month of the year. It is the Finder's responsibility to hire the right people to ensure financial statement accuracy.

B2B Adage: *Employees are often afraid to admit mistakes or to notify the Finder about bad news regarding the financial statements. These employees are concerned about their "job security" and will often withhold bad news until it is absolutely imperative, even to the detriment of the Finder.*

Timely Financial Statements

The internal financial statements of a company need to be issued monthly, preferably by the middle of the next month.

Calculate Income Taxes Monthly

It is very simple to calculate income taxes monthly when a company has timely and accurate financial statements.

Most privately held companies are pass-through entities for income tax reporting. **That often means that income from one company can be offset with losses from another, provided there is sufficient basis in the company that has incurred the loss.**

> **B2B Adage:** *Many Finders become very frustrated on April 15th because they discover, at the last moment, that the losses in one company can't be used to offset income in a different related-party company.*

It is in the best interest of a business owner to be shown, each month, the approximate amount of income taxes that will be owed on April 15th. Business owners should then be able to know the amount of cash that needs to be set aside to pay estimated income taxes.

> **B2B Adage:** *There should never be negative surprises to a Finder on April 15th.*

Verification from Your Independent Tax CPA

An owner should have a competent independent CPA verify the internally-projected income taxes at least once a quarter. This simple process can give them some peace of mind regarding April 15th. This quarterly update should not cost much money if the internal financial statements are accurate and timely. Additionally, the tax CPA might be able to advise on important tax matters on a timely basis.

Black Cloud #4 – Overtime

There are few companies that do not make errors in overtime calculations. The penalties for making errors in overtime can be severe.

Overtime is governed by the Fair Labor Standards Act (FLSA) and was approved by Congress in 1938. It is stunning to me that a law created so long ago is unfamiliar and misunderstood by Finders today.

It is not unusual for me to be hired by a company and discover that the company is in violation of the FLSA. The violation is often in the form of paying a person a "salary." When bringing the issue up to a Finder, the usual response is that the person should not be paid overtime because they are on a salary. Finders often become frustrated when they learn there are rules that require payment of overtime, even if a person is paid a salary.

B2B Adage: *A company may be responsible for overtime, even if an employee is paid a salary.*

There are certain exemptions for executive, administrative, professional, outside sales, or computer employees. However, the reasons for those exemptions must be known and documented. These exclusions can be very complicated and difficult to administer.

There are also rules that require overtime with a commissioned sales staff. The rules are somewhat complicated but are not worth the risk of violating.

The FLSA has made the following statement:

> "An employer who requires or permits an employee to work overtime is generally required to pay the employee premium pay for such overtime work. Employees covered by the Fair Labor Standards Act (FLSA) must receive overtime pay for hours worked in excess of 40 in a workweek of at least one and one-half times their regular rates of pay. The FLSA does not require overtime pay for work on Saturdays, Sundays, holidays, or regular days of rest, unless overtime hours are worked on such days. The FLSA, with some exceptions, requires bonus payments to be included as part of an employee's regular rate of pay in computing overtime." [33]

I have participated in numerous Department of Labor (DOL) audits during my career. Typically, I have been brought into the company after the overtime laws and regulations have been allegedly violated.

Regrettably, the DOL often has more power than the Internal Revenue Service. Their compliance information is well documented; however, it is often very difficult for a business owner to understand the DOL laws and regulations without a very competent human resources expert.

An owner and I attended a wrap-up meeting with the DOL on a particular engagement that I had been brought into regarding a DOL audit. The DOL thoroughly explained the fines and penalties. They also explained the deadline on which the monies had to be paid. They surprised the business owner with a $50,000 fine in addition to the other monies that were owed. The business owner got very upset and pleaded his case, but did not change the mind of the DOL auditor. The business owner left the room. I asked the auditor why the DOL issued the $50,000 fine. Quite unemotionally, the auditor said, "This law has been in place since 1938 and the owner should have taken the responsibility to know the law."

> **B2B Adage:** *The Department of Labor is powerful. Business owners should understand and comply with the laws, some of which have existed since 1938.*

Black Cloud #5 – Being Held Hostage

Invariably, when engaged with a company, I will sit down with the Finder and explain that certain employees have the ability to hold the company hostage. This means that certain employees have so much knowledge or so many responsibilities that, if they were to leave the company, the act of leaving would cause serious damage to the company. I have seen employees who, understanding this hostage-holding advantage, have created situations where they negotiated salary and benefits that exceed the market for their particular skills.

This is hostage-taking by the Finder's employee and the Finder is often afraid of reprimanding, terminating or disciplining the employee because of possible negative consequences to the company.

The keys to correcting this situation are to identify the potential hostage-holding situation and hire someone to create an infrastructure around the situation. In other words, internal controls and other systems need to be in place so the company can continue to function if the person was to leave the company, either voluntarily or involuntarily.

> **B2B Adage:** *Hostage-holding by one of your employ-ees, whether voluntary or involuntary, is detrimental to any company.*

Black Cloud #6 – The Balance Sheet

I truly enjoy visiting with Finders. I become motivated by their intelligence, drive and ambition.

One of the peculiar things about a Finder is that they can always tell me their personal net worth. If we are talking over lunch about this subject, the Finder can grab a napkin and write his or her estimated net worth within a few minutes. They know the value of their homes, their mortgage and the other assets they own. They have a keen ability to keep numbers in their heads and know their major personal assets and liabilities.

On the other hand, Finders often react differently when discussing the subject of the owner's equity that is listed on the company's balance sheet. Finders typically make statements about this document, such as, "I don't understand the balance sheet," or "I see no reason to look at the balance sheet," or "I know the balance sheet is wrong, so there is no reason for me to get involved," or "The balance sheet is not important to me because it does not show the true value of my assets."

There are numerous reasons why it is imperative for an owner to understand their company's balance sheet. A few of the key reasons are:

1. The assets and liabilities of the company are on this page. It is very important for an owner to understand what the company owns in assets and what it owes in liabilities.

2. It is highly likely that a weak accounting infrastructure or weak accounting staff will cause errors on the balance sheet. It is important for an owner to be able to tell people that the owner knows about the errors and that they want the errors fixed. A Finder who does not understand the balance sheet runs the risk of employee theft and other detrimental issues.

3. A banker will closely analyze the company's balance sheet and will create key ratios mostly from the balance sheet. A Finder who is able to converse with a banker about the balance sheet will not only gain respect from the banker but might also be able to negotiate and understand banker's terms.

4. The balance sheet shows the equity an owner has in a company. It is important to know the equity basis of the company's value.

Black Cloud #7 – Employee Pay

The proper amount to pay an employee is a frustrating topic to Finders. Employees can now go online to see the salary that third parties estimate the employee should be paid. Employees are often anxious for a "review" meeting with a Finder in order to argue their position that they deserve a raise.

Rule of Thumb

A simple rule of thumb can be used to determine the amount an employee should be paid: Find the amount of money it will take to replace and train the employee. Unless unusual circumstances occur, employees should not be paid above market value.

B2B Adage: *Employee pay is dictated by the market.*

B2B Adage*: An employee who is paid above market will eventually leave the company.*

There are a few reasons that an employee who is being paid above market will eventually leave the company:

1. The Finder knows the employee is being overpaid. This fact is always in the back of the Finder's mind. Eventually, this will bother the Finder enough that a situation will be created to cause the employee to leave the company.

2. Employees know when they are overpaid and are smart enough to know when a Finder is creating an infrastructure process that will expose the inflated salary. When this infrastructure creation is near completion, the employee will often start a job search and find a job with a different company in lieu of being asked to take a pay cut. Sometimes, the employee leaves to work for a competitor.

It is recommended that a Finder pay employees what the market will bear, and nothing more than that amount. Rather than a raise it might be wise to consider giving periodic bonuses to reward outstanding or exceptional behavior and/or results. Any bonus given to an employee should acknowledge that (1) the bonus is for a specific event or period of time and (2) any future bonuses will be discretionary and may or may not occur. A bonus process might prevent salaries from increasing to the point where employees are overpaid for the services rendered to the company.

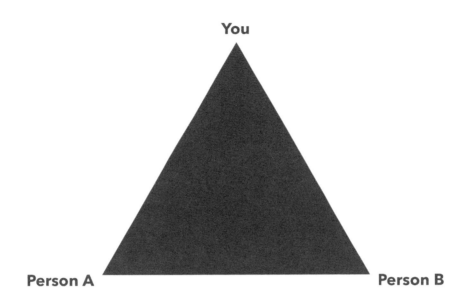

You

Person A　　　　　　　　　　　　Person B

CHAPTER 18

Triangular Relationships

Business owners often find themselves in triangular relationships. This chapter deals with these phenomena and suggests ways to avoid or escape them.

> **B2B Adage:** *Finders often unintentionally find themselves in triangular relationships.*

Relationships

Merriam Webster Dictionary defines a relationship as, "a state of affairs existing between those having shared dealings."

The adage "It's not what you know but who you know" is one of the best jewels of wisdom of the ages.

The best Finders are those who know how to build long-term relationships. Those relationships are typically the foundation of the Finding activities, as discussed earlier in this book. A business relationship typically starts between two people and looks like the following:

You ⟷ **Person A**

You and Person A spend time together in a mutually beneficial business relationship. As is the case with all relationships, there is some give-and-take as you both work toward your mutual goals.

A Triangular Relationship

A triangular relationship occurs when a third person (Person B) is brought into the relationship with you and Person A. The relationship of the three of you now looks something like the following:

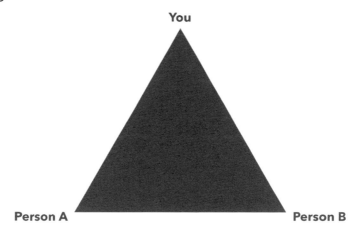

So far, there is nothing wrong with the relationship among the three of you. You all work well together; the lines of communication are open and there is a mutually beneficial and healthy business relationship among the three parties. This relationship works as long as the communication lines look something like the following:

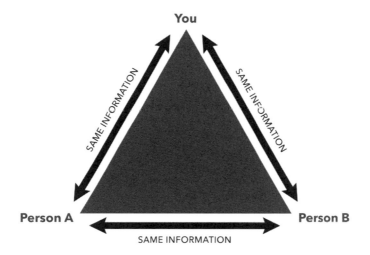

The trouble begins when the communication among the three parties breaks down and one or more legs of the triangle become imbalanced. The imbalance is typically caused by either (1) not properly communicating or (2) by communicating different information among the three parties. The communication lines then start to look something like the following:

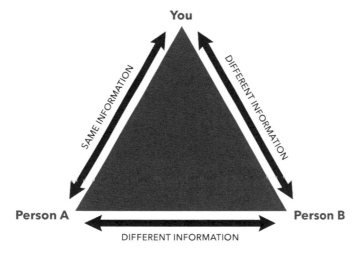

An Example – The Family

> "Dad comes home from work to find Mom coming down hard on Junior with "clean up your room or else," threats. Dad immediately comes to the rescue. "Mom," he might say, "Give the boy a break." Perhaps Mom, feeling victimized by Dad, turns on him, automatically moving in to a victim position. They might do a few quick trips around the triangle with Junior on the sidelines. Or maybe Junior joins Dad in a persecutory "let's gang up on Mom" approach, and they could play it from that angle. Or Junior could turn-coat on Dad, rescuing Mom, with: "Mind your own business, Dad ... I don't need your help!" So, it goes, with endless variations perhaps, but none-theless, round and round the triangle." [34]

And so, it goes in business. Finders can inadvertently create triangular relationships that harm the business, just as certain triangular relationships harm families.

Let's illustrate a couple of the most common types of this phenomenon in business—multiple owners of a privately held company and nepotism.

Co-owners of a Business

Co-owners often inadvertently cause triangular relationships with employees, vendors, bankers, customers and a host of people. This sometimes occurs in situations such as the following:

- **The co-owners do not have the same information.**

  The source of information and the methods of communication between co-owners are critical. They must have identical information from accounting, vendors, bankers, employees and customers. They must also meet often to discuss the information received from the variety of sources to make sure everyone comprehends the information the same. Otherwise, they risk creating triangular relationships.

- **The co-owners can become irritated with each other**.

  The co-owners may not like, trust or respect each other. Sometimes, the irritation leads to the relationship's deterioration. This situation is bad when the change in relationship is understood between the co-owners. This situation becomes dangerous when only one of the co-owners understands the change in the relationship. What occurs in this case is that Owner A will start communicating with other people instead of talking with Owner B. The new triangular relationship now looks something like this:

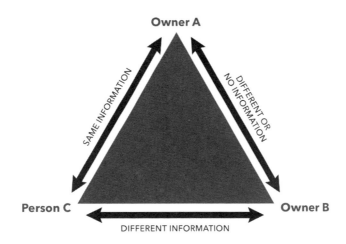

This is a Dangerous Situation!

No good can possibly result from this change in relationships, as is illustrated in the above diagram. This is a lose-lose situation for the owners, but it puts Person C in an insecure position. Person C is forced to start "taking sides" with one of the owners. Owner A will typically go to Person C and say something such as, "Don't tell Owner B, but I have decided to …."

In this situation, Owner A is not only looking out for his or her own best interests but is putting Person C in a precarious situation. The Person C's of the world, if they are employees, often become stressed over this type of a change in the triangular relationship. They often feel like they are asked to lie or keep secrets. They then spend time discussing the situation with their spouse and/ or other people. They feel they are painted into a corner and start to worry if they will get in trouble with Owner B.

Another danger of the above example is that Person C (employee, vendor, banker, or customer) often begins to question Owner A's judgement.

Person C often thinks or says (to others) something like, "If Owner A is going to do this to one of his partners, I wonder when he or she is going to do the same to me." Person C's defense mechanisms then kick in. Person C starts to withdraw from both Owner A and Owner B. Person C hopes that Owner A will stop sharing this information and, simultaneously, hopes that Owner B will never discover the "secret" that has been shared. Person C has unnecessary burdens placed upon his or her back. These burdens are bothersome and stressful, and they eventually take a toll. The toll may not be worth the cost to Owner A or Owner B.

> **B2B Adage:** *Co-owners should either communicate very well with each other or end the business relationship.*

There are only two solutions to correct the communication lines between two co-owners:

- They agree to communicate with each other, in spite of their changed feelings;

- Or they agree to end the relationship by creating an exit strategy for one of the owners.

Nepotism

Nepotism is a peculiar source of triangular relationships that often causes damage in a company.

Merriam-Webster Dictionary tells us the word is derived from the Latin word nepot and is defined as:

> Favoritism shown to a relative (as by giving an appointive job).

Most of an owner's employees regard the word "nepotism" as a four-letter word, although they will never say this to an owner's face. The nepotistic triangular relationship may look something like the following:

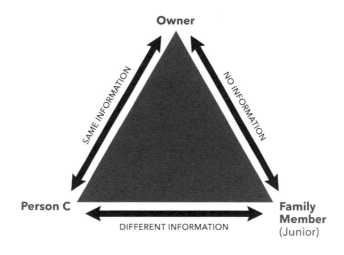

The trouble with hiring a family member is that person C always assumes nepotism exists, whether or not that is the case. The owner will typically try to avoid any conflict with Junior and will sit down with Person C and demand that he or she confront Junior. This puts Person C in a bad situation because Person C is smart enough to know the adage, "blood is thicker than water" and assumes that bad things are going to occur.

A simple way to explain the problem is to describe a peculiar weakness that Finders have in running their business—that of delegating responsibility without giving the authority.

Responsibility vs. Authority

Finders are good at delegating responsibilities. This is a natural part of their personalities and is a key component of what makes them a Finder.

B2B Adage: *Finders are good at delegating responsibility but are often bad at giving authority.*

We quickly get to the root of the problem with nepotism. The Finder delegates to Person C the responsibility to shape up Junior **without giving the authority to person C to fire or reprimand Junior.**

Person C knows he or she has been given the responsibility but not the authority, creating a lose-lose situation between Person C and the owner. Person C's defense mechanisms kick into gear. This person may begin to sugarcoat instructions with Junior hoping that Junior will not go home and tell Mom or Dad that Person C has been unfair. Person C knows that Junior may not be above exaggerating things said by Person C at the business to Mom or Dad.

In fact, Person C suspects that Junior is good at playing Mom and Dad against each other. Hence, we often see a double triangular relationship that looks like the following:

Person 1	Person 2	Person 3
The Owner	Person C	Junior
Mom	Person C	Junior

Fellow employees may begin to talk or laugh behind the back of the owner and/or Junior. Employees may begin to let some rules slide when it comes to Junior with the hope that they will not be reprimanded by Junior's Mom or Dad.

> **B2B Adage**: *Family members should be treated like any other employee.*

No good can result from showing favoritism to a family member.

Here are some potential consequences:

1. The owner is harmed because Junior does not learn the discipline necessary to become a productive employee.

2. Junior does not learn the skills necessary to properly lead or productively work in the company in the future.

3. Junior does not earn the respect of the employees of the company and becomes unqualified to lead the company in the future.

4. Employees become demoralized by nepotism and lose respect for both the owner and the family member.

5. Key employees begin to look for an exit strategy from the company in order to avoid Junior and the future confrontations that will likely occur.

   B2B Adage: *Family members should perform better for the company than regular employees. Family members should be fired if they perform below average.*

An owner should consider paying family members the going market rate for the services they provide to the company.

Get out of Triangular Relationships

If a Finder becomes aware of this kind of a situation, they will eventually recognize a triangular relationship and will voluntarily leave the situation. A good way to do this is to sit down with the party that is causing the triangular relationship and calmly express the desire to be removed from the relationship. If this does not work, you might need to consider removing yourself from the relationship permanently. Let me give you an example.

I was hired a few years ago by the personal representative of a business owner who had been brutally murdered. The personal representative became the new CEO of the company previously owned by the victim. The company's employees worked in multiple states and the company had between 80 and 100 employees. The new CEO and I worked together for a couple of years to try to save the company. Sadly, the company had been left with too much debt.

When the company filed for Chapter 11 bankruptcy the court gave the secured creditors a significant amount of power to control the destiny of the company. The power of the secured creditors exceeded the power of the new CEO.

A meeting was eventually held with the attorneys and other representatives of the secured creditors and the new CEO. I was asked to attend the meeting. The representatives of the secured creditors began to make demands of me that were simply not acceptable.

I could very easily have provided the information requested; however, the relationship changed to a degree that I was put in a position of reporting to the secured creditors instead of the new CEO. I immediately saw the triangular relationship that was about to form. I wisely left the meeting and immediately resigned. In that situation, I did not create the triangular relationship but had the power to remove myself from the situation.

Do yourself a favor; recognize when you are in or are creating triangular relationships. Then, either stop or remove yourself from the triangular relationship.

> **B2B Adage:** *There is never a win-win-win in a bad triangular relationship. The only permanent solution is to fix it or remove oneself from such a situation.*

CHAPTER 19

Your Exit from Your Company

Note: This chapter is from our proprietary book, *Avoiding the Danger Zone, Business Illusions*. The following has been included in this book because Finders who escape or avoid **The Danger Zone** will eventually contemplate the topic of selling or transferring their companies. This chapter gives foundational advice to Finders before they begin this journey.

Have you considered what it will be like the day after you exit your company?

The editors of *Strategies Magazine* asked me to write an article on the subject of exit strategies for business owners. Below is an excerpt from the article:

"Benjamin Franklin is credited with the adage, 'In this world nothing is certain but death and taxes.'

That statement is as true today as it was when he wrote it more than 200 years ago. We can add another adage for today's business owners: You will exit your company one day in the future.

Your exit from your company may be planned or unplanned. The exit may bring satisfaction or dissatisfaction to you and your family. It may be to the benefit or detriment of your employees or associates. It may bring great financial reward, or it may bring financial devastation.

The exit may bring fame or shame to your family and friends. It may be the continuance or discontinuance of the company you have worked so hard to build and create. The exit may be to the benefit or detriment of your competitors. Regardless of the consequences, you will someday exit your company in one form or another." [35]

And, so it will be with you. Regardless of your intentions or desires, the day will come when you are no longer the owner of your business.

YOU CAN TAKE MY COMPANY AND...

Some of you may want to leave your company right now. I can almost hear some of you say, *"You can take my company and ..."* I have heard that sentiment more than once during my career.

I believe all of us as business owners have experienced the highs and lows of owning a company and have vacillated from desires of trashing the entire company to keeping it and selling it for millions.

It is tempting to quit too early. Too often a business owner will travel 90% of the journey and then sell the business. Yet, there is a strong possibility that the value earned during the last 10% of the journey could be worth more than the first 90%.

What are your desires for exiting your company? Do you want to pass it on to family members? Do you want to sell it to employees or a third party? Do you want to quit and liquidate the assets into cash? Do you want to work at your business until the day you die and not think about what will happen to the company after your death?

EXIT EXPECTATIONS

I often ask business owners, "What amount of money do you want to receive for your company upon your exit?"

Their answers are very interesting and range from the logical to the unreasonable. But most owners have given some thought to the matter and have a certain amount of money they feel their company is worth or what they want upon their exit. Most can give me a relative range and might say something like, "I believe my company is worth at least 20 million dollars."

Getting owners to tell me what they want for their business is the easy part. Having them explain why their companies are worth that amount of money is much more difficult. After all, the owners are emotionally tied to the companies and are not objective about their value. In fact, seldom can owners tell me the true value of their companies they wish to sell.

Some owners undervalue their company. It is almost as if they are so involved in the day-to-day grind of the business that they do not have the time to step back and see what a remarkable job they have done in actually creating and running them.

Others have unrealistic expectations about what they will get for their businesses. They might have a gut feeling of what their companies are worth but they tend to gloss over certain flaws in their companies that will bring down their value.

In reality, preparing to sell your business is like preparing to sell your home. Perhaps your home is worth a lot of money, and you want to sell it at a certain price. It's structure and square footage are appealing to prospects, but your real estate professional points out that you could improve your profits significantly by doing some painting, landscaping or repairs. Your choice then becomes whether or not to invest a little more money to improve your house so you can maximize your profits when it is sold.

The same can be said for selling a business. It is worth something today, but what can you do in the future to make it worth even more so you can sell it at a higher price?

THE CHECK

Ultimately, the value of your company is only worth what someone else will pay for it. This is often a cold reality to business owners, but it is indeed reality. If you want a certain amount of money for your business, then you must do what it takes to have someone open their checkbook and write a check for that amount. Unrealistic hoping will not get you the check, but methodical planning and investing might.

A part of your job in getting the check will be to find the people who have the ability to write it. You may need to develop relationships with people who can help you find a buyer.

Victory will go to the aggressor, and the aggressor should get busy developing relationships that will eventually lead to a check—that is, a check for the right amount of money.

GOAL CLARITY

One of my favorite authors is Ron Willingham. Ron gave advice that will help you reach your exit strategy goals. He stated the following about goal clarity:

> "This means having clear, specific, written goals of what you want to happen in your future. They must be goals that you deeply desire and, most important, goals you firmly believe are possible for you to achieve and that you feel you deserve to achieve." [36]

What are the "clear, specific, written goals" that you want to achieve when you exit your company? Do you truly desire them and feel you deserve them? Are they possible? Have you written them down? And if you haven't, would you consider taking time to do this over the next few days?

EMOTIONAL INTELLIGENCE

One thing that often frustrates entrepreneurs is the realization that they are alone in the organization in their concerns regarding the future of the company. This is one of the reasons for the adage, "It's lonely at the top." Entrepreneurs need to realize that, with few exceptions, nobody will ever really understand or empathize with that loneliness.

Discouragement is a natural feeling we experience while we go through the ebbs and flows of business cycles. We often feel we are pulling a weight that exceeds our capacity.

We sometimes become angry at others or our situation. Anger is not a primary emotion—it is a secondary one. When we feel sad, hurt or betrayed, we often feel anger. The anger will pass, and we will get back to our natural optimistic selves if we keep the long-term picture in perspective.

I find my attitude improves when I read good books. The wisdom of the ages is in print, and it brings much comfort to my soul to learn that I am not alone with many of the emotions I feel on my journey. Ron Willingham addresses the issue of rising to a level to understand our emotions as we pass through the inevitable difficulties of our journey. He defined a term he calls "emotional intelligence."

"Emotional Intelligence – This is basically two things: It's the ability to understand the emotions you're feeling and their impact on your behavior. It helps you identify fear of rejection and its numerous emotional cousins that, if allowed to rule your actions, can kill your success. Emotional intelligence gives you the self-management skills to deal with negative emotions, natural resistance to change, fear of rejection, temporary defeats, and other success killers.

It's having the inner strength to do the necessary activities that you don't want to do, but must do in order to be successful. It's also the will power or emotional endurance to work through all the ups and downs that come your way."[37]

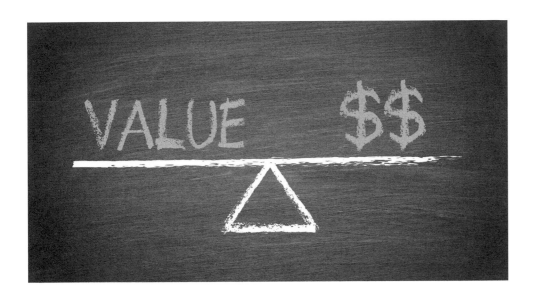

CHAPTER 20

Note: This chapter is a natural transition from the previous one and is from our proprietary book, *The Exit Strategy Handbook*. That book discloses our survey in which we discovered the concerns of Finders about selling their businesses. Approximately 62% are concerned about value and sales price. Any Finder who considers selling or transferring a business needs to know the following information to be in control of this important process.

The Realistic Value of Your Business

"You can increase the value of your business if you understand how buyers are likely to value it."[38]

Frederick D. Lipman

"Any profitable business can be sold. It's just a matter of value, terms and structure. Total company value is not always equal to the cash received at the close of the sale of the business."

Larry Reinharz, Managing Director, Woodbridge International

This chapter will give you and *The Success Team*™ the tools to arrive at a realistic value of your business. (The roles of this team are explained in our proprietary book, *The Exit Strategy Handbook.)* These tools will also be able to be used to determine if the value of your business materially increases or decreases during the exit strategy process.

Determining the realistic value of your business can be one of the most difficult topics during the exit strategy process. Business owners often feel:

1. Buyers and appraisers are intentionally undervaluing the business

2. The prospective buyer does not really understand the true value of the business

3. The various valuation methods are not realistic ways to calculate value

4. Not enough value is given to intangibles, such as employees and customers.

DIFFERENT VALUATION METHODS

The process of placing a consistent dollar value on your business can be very frustrating. One of the frustrations is that there are numerous ways that buyers and appraisers use to value a business.

Some appraisers use two or more valuation methods within the same report, which can be very irritating. Below are some of the most common valuation methods:

1. EBITDA Method
2. Discounted Cash Flow Method
3. Comparable Company Method of Valuation
4. Comparable Transaction Method of Valuation
5. Asset Accumulation Method
6. Acquisition Debt Value
7. Liquidation Value [39]

YOUR COMPANY'S BALANCE SHEET

Your company's balance sheet has assets, tangible and intangible, that may be of value to the future buyer. Those assets will be valued using certain methods sometime before the purchase. The process in this chapter will not calculate the value of those assets. Rather, their value will be deferred to the future until your company is closer to bringing in a potential buyer.

The buyer will determine which of your company's assets it wants to purchase. Be prepared that the buyer may not be interested in purchasing some of your company's assets, such as your building.

BALANCE SHEET ERRORS

It has been our experience that almost all companies have material errors on their balance sheets. These errors are often compounded if the company owns subsidiary companies. These errors may have a significant impact on the valuation process to be explained below. It is critical to fix any potential errors on the balance sheet prior to going through the valuation process explained in this chapter.

THE EBITDA METHOD

> "A number of businesses are valued by buyers based upon accounting earnings or income. Indeed, one of the most common methods of valuation is the so-called EBITDA method. This involves the determination of your accounting earnings before interest, taxes, depreciation, and amortization (EBITDA), and multiplication of the EBITDA by the relevant multiplier to obtain a business valuation." [40]
>
> *Frederick D. Lipman*

> "The main indicator of value, to a PEG (Private Equity Group), or other buyer, is earnings before interest, taxes, depreciation and amortization, or EBITDA. EBITDA is a framework that allows buyers to compare "apples to apples" instead of 'apples to oranges. when viewing businesses with different operating structures." [41]
>
> *Robert W. Scarlata*

> "For each $1 that you increase your EBITDA during the valuation year, you should arguably receive an additional $4 to $6 in sale price." [42]

This chapter will illustrate several steps to the valuation of your company using the EBITDA method along with an explanation of these steps:

1. The EBITDA calculation
2. Adjustments to EBITDA
3. EBITDA multipliers

4. The format for the adjusted EBITDA valuation
5. EBITDA valuation periods

THE EBITDA CALCULATION

The calculations below assume two types of companies: taxable and pass-through. A taxable entity is a C-Corporation. Pass-through entities are typically S-Corporations, limited liability companies (LLC), partnerships or sole proprietorships.

DESCRIPTION	TAXABLE ENTITY	PASS-THROUGH ENTITY
Revenue	$9,000,000	$9,000,000
Cost of sales	6,000,000	6,000,000
Gross profit	3,000,000	3,000,000
Administrative expense	1,900,000	1,900,000
Income before taxes	1,100,000	1,100,000
Income taxes	440,000	-
Income after taxes	$660,000	$1,100,000
EBITDA calculation		
Income after taxes, above	$660,000	$1,100,000
Interest expense	180,000	180,000
Income taxes	440,000	-
Depreciation expense	105,000	105,000
Amortization expenses	15,000	15,000
EBITDA	$1,400,000	$1,400,000

ADJUSTMENTS TO EBITDA

The difficult part of using EBITDA as a valuation method is the identification of adjustments to EBITDA, which are usually items that might be considered distortions to the EBITDA calculation by prospective buyers. *The Success Team*™ needs to spend time identifying and discussing any possible adjustment to EBITDA long before an examination is performed by independent CPAs and before any discussion with prospective buyers.

> "Your EBITDA is then adjusted to remove expenses and revenue that will no longer be carried forward into the new business. These adjustments can be quite substantial for a closely held family business.
>
> Most closely held businesses are operated to minimize income taxes. As a result, excessive compensation and perquisites may be provided to the owner and his family in order to reduce taxes. The excessive compensation and perquisites are really forms of disguised dividends." [43]

Frederick D. Lipman

"One of the most frequent errors in performing this kind of an analysis to take the EBITDA or EBIT numbers at face value, without considering whether these numbers really reflect the true economic performance of your company.

Your financial statements will seldom reflect the real economic performance of your company. Numerous distortions may creep in." [44]

Les Nemethy

It is important to understand that *The Success Team*™ and a prospective buyer are not judging your business acumen on the decisions you have made on certain expenses in the Income Statement. Rather, they are trying to evaluate what the EBITDA of the company might be under normal circumstances. The prospective buyers are also trying to compare your company to similar types of companies in order to determine which company, if any, they might want to purchase. It is very important to be open with the members of *The Success Team*™ and to not take personal offense during the discussion. The goal of *The Success Team*™ is to help you through a most difficult process.

Some business owners face the issues of income tax avoidance and income tax evasion during this process.

As a way to illustrate this subject of adjustments to EBITDA, let's look at a potential adjustment that would be a decrease to EBITDA.

"The owner/manager of Company A draws no salary from the company. His market salary would be $200,000 per year, or $250,000 grossed up with all payroll and social security taxes. If an investor was to buy this business, the former owner/manager would presumably not be prepared to stay and work for free indefinitely; nor would a replacement be willing to work for free. Presumably the new managers would ask for a market salary. Hence EBITDA and EBIT (Earnings before interest and taxes) would be diminished by $250,000." [45]

This example makes sense. You would do the same if you were considering purchasing a company. You would look at the Income Statement to see if the owner/manager had not been deducting a salary. Your first reaction would be something like, "It will cost me at least $250,000 to replace this guy, so I am going to lower my offer to this company because of my future costs that are not currently recorded in this company's expenses."

This is not a judgment of your business acumen. Rather, it is a prudent analysis by a prudent potential buyer about the future increase in operational costs of your business. This is merely a business decision that must be made by the prospective buyer. It is also a business analysis that should be considered by *The Success Team*™.

Below is an example of an adjustment that would be an increase to EBITDA.

> "The son of the owner/manager of Company B is 17 years old and is working part-time for Company B, drawing a salary of $100,000 (fully grossed up). The son is not producing anything of value for Company B, nor would the investor wish to continue with the son on the payroll. In this case, EBITDA and EBITDA would be increased by $100,000." [46]

Some owners can get a bit extravagant in their expenses to the company.

> "The owner of Company C purchased four helicopters. This was not at all necessary for operation of the company's core business (This has actually happened!). The $450,000 required for the operation of the helicopters should be added back to EBITDA and EBIT."[47]

Some business owners can become very creative on the topic of writing off personal expense in the company's Income Statement:

> "I know a businessman in Texas who writes off almost $10,000 annually on his personal "work boots." He really does purchase the boots, but they tend to come in exotic leathers like ostrich and boa constrictor, and he seldom wears them to work."[48]

Below is a list of potential discretionary items in the Income Statement that may be adjustments to EBITDA. These adjustments may be either increases or decreases to EBITDA and may have a material impact on the valuation of the business:

1. Excessive compensation to owners, management or employees
2. Personal legal costs for estate planning, divorce, or other litigation
3. No income or below-market income to owners or management
4. Tuition and educational expenses for children or family members
5. Cash donations to charitable organizations
6. Golf, country club or other such expenses not really necessary to the business
7. Nepotism expenses (such as salary, autos, computers or vacations to family members)
8. Vacations or other related party travel expenses, including time-share expenses
9. Multiple vehicles or unusual vehicle expenses for the owner, or their family
10. Excessive insurance to owners and related parties (e.g., life, health or disability)
11. Building rent paid to an owner that is in excess of or under market value
12. Equipment leases paid to an owner that are in excess of or under market value
13. Professional sports tickets not necessary for the business
14. Rental expenses or repairs that would normally be paid by a landlord
15. Jewelry, antique cards or other such lavish hobbies
16. Below-market transfers of assets to related parties or family members
17. Discounted sales prices to related parties
18. Costs paid in excess of market to vendors who are related parties or friends
19. Discounts or free delivery given to related parties or friends

20. Repairs, remodeling, maintenance, insurance or other expenses for a personal residence
21. Inventory or scrap sold in cash and not deposited into the company's bank account
22. Alimony or child-support payments made by the company
23. Bonuses or other perks that are above-market costs

Not all adjustments are discretionary items such as the above examples. Some adjustments are one-time or otherwise unusual expenses.

> "My company negotiated the sale of a business that was operating a large fleet of trucks. Suddenly, fuel prices shot up to unprecedented levels. We assessed the situation and found reason to believe that fuel prices would be more stable in the future. In preparing the profit and loss statement for EBITDA purposes, we recast the most recent fuel costs to more reasonable levels."[49]

> *Robert W. Scarlata*

Below are examples of one-time, nonrecurring or unusual expenses that might be included in adjusted EBITDA:

1. Maintenance capital expenditures
2. IT capital expenditures
3. Write-off of an unproductive or obsolete asset
4. Unusual, one-time or prior period adjustments proposed by independent CPAs
5. Legal expenses incurred for the exit strategy
6. Legal costs of restructuring or reorganization
7. Audit, appraisal or consulting fees for the exit strategy
8. Litigation expenses that have concluded and are nonrecurring
9. Costs of exits of minority owners prior to the sale of the company
10. Insurance claims
11. Opening a new facility
12. Writing off inventory that is unusual or nonrecurring
13. Unusual bad-debt expenses, such as a Chapter 11 bankruptcy filing by a customer
14. Employment costs, such as large severance or other nonrecurring expenses
15. Large and unusual bonuses or other compensation paid for nonrecurring transactions
16. Differences between book and tax depreciation
17. Professional fees, such as creating a Defined Contribution or Benefit Plan
18. Leases that were expensed instead of being capitalized
19. Equipment that was expensed instead of being capitalized
20. One-time marketing, branding, public relations or research costs

In short, *The Success Team*™ should carefully comb through the Costs of Sales, Selling, General, Administrative or other expense categories to determine if there are one-time, nonrecurring or unusual expenses in the Income Statement. As a rule of thumb: When in doubt, disclose the item and place it in adjusted EBITDA.

EBITDA MULTIPLIERS

Once adjusted, EBITDA needs to be multiplied by a certain range of numbers that are called "multipliers." These numbers are used to help with the estimated valuation of your business.

> "The adjusted EBITDA is then multiplied by a multiplier to obtain an overall valuation for the business (also called "enterprise value"). The multiplier typically ranges from 4 to 6 times adjusted EBITDA, particularly for financial buyers. However, the multiplier has gone below 4 and substantially above 6, depending upon whether it is a buyer's market or a seller's market for the sale of businesses. A multiplier above 6 is more typical for strategic rather than financial buyers.
>
> Multipliers of 20 or more are not unheard of for strategic buyers of companies with strong market niches.

The multipliers are derived from comparable company valuations, including the multipliers applicable to public companies in the same industry. For example, if a public company in your industry has a total market valuation (based on its stock price) of 10 times its EBITDA, this multiplier could be the starting point in determining the appropriate multiplier.

This multiplier would then be discounted by the fact that your company was smaller and has less market dominance.

Many business owners incorrectly assume that the multipliers applicable to larger companies in the industry apply to their smaller company. The multipliers for less dominant companies in an industry are significantly smaller than for dominant companies." [50]

The multiplier used for your company will depend much upon whether you sell during a buyer's or seller's market.

Below is one author's (*Rick Rickertsen* [51]) view of the different levels of multipliers to be applied to adjusted EBITDA.

EXAMPLE OF EBITDA MULTIPLIERS

Option	Multiple
Strategic Buyer	8-10x
Private Equity (Financial Buyer)	6-8x
Management Buyout (MBO)	5-7x
ESOP	5-6x

This topic should be discussed by the members of *The Success Team*™ in order to find the estimated multipliers relevant to your business during the exit planning process.

ADJUSTED EBITDA AND THE VALUATION CALCULATION

The following is a fictitious illustration of ABC Example Company, Inc. *The Success Team*™ has worked together to find the adjustments to EBITDA and the appropriate estimated multiplier. They have already calculated EBITDA and will begin to add or subtract the adjustments. They will then use the agreed-upon estimated multiplier of five times adjusted EBITDA to arrive at the estimated value of the business.

DESCRIPTION	AMOUNT
EBITDA	**$795,000**
Additions:	
Legal, reorganization, audit and appraisal costs to prepare for the sale	165,000
Salaries of family members that will not continue with the buyer	125,000
One-time bonuses paid for a nonrecurring and unusual transaction	75,000
Officer life and disability insurance that will not continue after the sale	25,000
Legal and other costs to buy out a minority owner of the company	80,000
Country club fees and season tickets to the Chicago Cubs	25,000
Vehicles, education and other expenses for three family members	45,000
Deductions:	
Increase in the cost of the person that will replace the owner/manager	(50,000)
Rent paid to the owner below market value for anequivalent building	(45,000)
Below-market salaries paid to key employees to continue with the buyer	(40,000)
Adjusted EBITDA	**$1,200,000**
Multiplier	5x
Estimated value of ABC Example Company, Inc.	**$6,000,000**

EBITDA VALUATION PERIODS

The Success Team™ will need to discuss the periods of time for the adjusted EBITDA calculations. There are several options:

1. The past 36 months
2. Trailing 24-month period
3. Trailing 12-month period
4. Weighted three-year period

It is highly recommended that you begin the process of calculating the current value of your company immediately.

CHAPTER 21

An inspiring Quote for Finders

"It is lonely at the top" is an aphorism that has come up in this book. Only those of us who are true Finders understand this statement.

The following passage from James Allen's *As a Man Thinketh* lifts my spirits whenever I feel this loneliness. I wanted to give this pearl of great price its own chapter so it would stand out from the rest of the information in this book.

"The thoughtless, the ignorant, and the indolent, seeing only the apparent effects of things and not the things themselves, talk of luck, of fortune, and chance. Seeing a man grow rich, they say, 'How lucky he is!' Observing another become intellectual, they exclaim, 'How highly favored he is!' And noting the saintly character and wide influence of another, they remark, 'How chance aids him at every turn!'

"They do not see the trials and failures and struggles which these men have voluntarily encountered in order to gain their experience. They have no knowledge of the sacrifices they have made, of the undaunted efforts they have put forth, of the faith they have exercised, that they might overcome the apparently insurmountable, and realize the Vision of their heart. They do not know the darkness and the heartaches; they only see the light and joy, and call it 'luck'; do not see the long and arduous journey but only behold the pleasant goal, and call it 'good fortune'; do not understand the process, but only perceive the result and call it 'chance.'

"In all human affairs there are *efforts*, and there are *results*, and the strength of the effort is the measure of the result. Chance is not. 'Gifts,' powers, material, intellectual and spiritual possessions are the fruit of effort. They are thoughts completed, objects accomplished, visions realized.

"The Vision that you glorify in your mind, the Ideal that you enthrone in your heart—this you will build your life by, this you will become."

"Law, not confusion, is the dominating principle in the universe. Justice, not injustice, is the soul and substance of life. This being so, man has but to right himself to find that the universe is right; and during the process of putting himself right, he will find that as he alters his thoughts towards things and other people, things and other people will alter toward him." [52]

CHAPTER 22

B2B CFO® Adages

An adage is a short statement expressing a general truth. Below are the adages from this book in chronological order as a quick reference guide.

1. You can't teach values to employees but you can find people who share your core values.

2. You want to get rid of anyone in your organization who does not share your core values. They should already have learned core values, such as honesty and good work ethic before joining your company.

3.   If you delegate responsibility without the authority, you will after a period of time, be given back the responsibility.

4.   Whether written or unwritten, the company's organizational chart exists today. The Finder's future success is dependent upon working properly within the rules of the informal organizational chart.

5.   Every company has an unofficial organizational chart, which is intentionally or unintentionally created by the business owner.

6.   It's lonely at the top. Don't expect anyone to understand or fully empathize with that loneliness.

7.   Finders live in the future with little regard to what has happened in the past.

8.   Finders evoke strong emotions from others, such as love or hate.

9.   There is no reason to try to be friends with everyone, because they are looking for a leader, not a friend.

10.   Minders live in the past and are not future thinkers.

11.   Finders are not good Minders.

12.   Most Finders started their careers as Grinders.

13.   Grinders are only concerned about what happens today. No concern is given about the past or the future.

14.   Far too many white-collar crimes committed by Minders are not reported to the legal authorities, which allows the Minder to steal from future employers.

15. Every company should have a current Policies and Procedures Employee Handbook. That HR manual should be updated any time a federal, state, or local law or regulation is changed.

16. Some business owners unintentionally place their employees in a position to steal from the company.

17. Do not rely upon your CPA firm to detect theft or fraud, unless you specifically engage them for this function for a specified period of time.

18. Most Finders do not spend a lot of time methodically planning their business infrastructure.

19. Far too often, company resources are spent in buying things that do not always lead to excellent customer service.

20. The failure to plan infrastructure will eventually hurt the company and will take away from finding customers at some point in the future.

21. Your competitors are actively planning today to take away your customers tomorrow.

22. **The Danger Zone** is created when the cash needs of a company far exceed the cash available to meet those needs.

23. We have yet to see a Finder with the desire or goal to start a business to spend time on accounting and computer problems, yet far too many spend too much time resolving those things.

24. The Finder must learn to trust people. Employees should be terminated from the company if they are not trustworthy.

25. Good management is defined as the accomplishment of the goals and objectives of the company through the actions of other people.

26. During **The Danger Zone,** the Finder hires sales people and senior level executives to help the company find cash.

27. Leaders make tough decisions. There is no benefit in shuffling chairs on the deck of the Titanic. Leaders look to the future and avoid the icebergs that are in the path of their company.

28. Computers in the future will be faster than computers you purchase today, which means you must have an active computer replacement plan.

29. A company that does not comply with Moore's Law (i.e., investing in technology and computer infrastructure, regardless of the industry) will be severely punished by this law.

30. A significant increase in sales sometimes means that the company might have a decrease in cash, which is the opposite of what Finders expect with sales increases.

31. Someone is spending time with your current and future different customer. If not you, it will be your competition.

32. Bad financial information typically leads to bad decision making.

33. If you expect to beat your competition, you must have better financial information infrastructure than your competition.

34. A Finder should never relinquish control of the company.

35. Many Finders spend too much energy worrying about the amount of money they will owe the IRS on April 15th.

36. Your company must have accurate financial statements in order to make accurate projections of the income taxes that will be owed on April 15th.

37. Employees are often afraid to admit mistakes or to notify the Finder about bad news regarding the financial statements. These employees are concerned about their "job security" and will often withhold bad news until it is absolutely imperative, even to the detriment of the Finder.

38. Many Finders become very frustrated on April 15th because they discover, at the last moment, that the losses in one company can't be used to offset income in a different related-party company.

39. There should never be negative surprises to a Finder on April 15th.

40. A company may be responsible for overtime, even if an employee is paid a salary.

41. The Department of Labor is powerful. Business owners should understand and comply with the laws, some of which have existed since 1938.

42. Hostage-holding by one of your employees, whether voluntary or involuntary, is detrimental to any company.

43. The Finder must understand the company's balance sheet.

44. Employee pay is dictated by the market.

45. An employee who is paid above market will eventually leave the company.

46. Finders often unintentionally find themselves in triangular relationships.

47. Co-owners should either communicate very well with each other or end the business relationship.

48. Finders are good at delegating responsibility but are often bad at giving authority.

49. Family members should be treated like any other employee.

50. Family members should perform better for the company than regular employees. Family members should be fired if they perform below average.

51. There is never a win-win-win in a bad triangular relationship. The only permanent solution is to fix it or remove oneself from such a situation.

REFERENCES

1. John Cook, *The Book of Positive Quotations*, 494.
2. James Allen, *As a Man Thinketh*, 50.
3. Stephen R. Covey, *The Seven Habits of Highly Effective People, 25ᵗʰ Anniversary Edition*, 147.
4. James C. Collins and Jerry I. Porras, *Built to Last*, 11.
5. Ibid., 73.
6. Ibid., 74-75.
7. Jim Collins, *Good to Great*, 195.
8. James C. Collins and Jerry I. Porras, *Built to Last*, 9.
9. Ibid., 70.
10. James Allen, *As a Man Thinketh*, 60.
11. Simon Sinek, *Start With Why*, 39.
12. Ibid., 41.
13. Phrase taught to the author by David Moore, Panamint Group.
14. Stephen R. Covey, *The Seven Habits of Highly Effective People, 25ᵗʰ Anniversary Edition*, 108.
15. Ibid., 108.
16. Thomas J. Stanley, Ph.D. and William D. Danko, Ph.D., *The Millionaire Next Door*, 240.
17. Jerry L. Mills, *Avoiding The Danger Zone, Business Illusions*, 47.
18. cnbc.com/2017/09/12/workplace-crime-costs-us-businesses-50-billion-a-year.html.
19. Terrence Darly Shulman, *Biting the Hand That Feeds, The Employee Theft Epidemic*, viii, 102.
20. Samuel Greengard, *Beating Back Fraud, Business Finance Magazine*, 02/06, 28.
21. Dictionary.com.
22. Britannica.com.
23. Gardner H. Russell, *The Effective Entrepreneur*, 99.

24. Napoleon Hill and W. Clement Stone, *Success Through a Positive Mental Attitude*, 155.

25. Stephen R. Covey, *The Seven Habits of Highly Effective People, 25th Anniversary Edition*, 50.

26. Investopedia.com/slide-show/top-6-reasons-new-businesses-fail.

27. Stephen R. Covey, *The Seven Habits of Highly Effective People, 25th Anniversary Edition*, 50.

28. Investopedia.com/terms/m/mooreslaw.asp.

29. Satish Kumar and Freddie Whitefield, *Visionaries: The 20th Century's 100 Most Important Inspirational Leaders*, 94.

30. Bo Birlingham, *Finish Big*, 70.

31. Jerry L. Mills, *The Exit Strategy Handbook*, 46.

32. Ibid., 59.

33. Dol.gov/general/topic/wages/overtimepay.

34. metafilter.com/32217/Triangular-relationships.

35. Jerry L. Mills, *Avoiding The Danger Zone*, Business Illusions, 4-5.

36. Ron Willingham, *Integrity Selling for the 21st Century*, 2.

37. Ibid., 3.

38. Fredrick D. Lipman, *The Complete Guide to Valuing & Selling Your Business*, 10.

39. Ibid., 14,18,21-23,26-27.

40. Ibid., 14.

41. Robert W. Scarlata, *Manage to Sell Your Business*, 89-90.

42. Fredrick D. Lipman, *The Complete Guide to Valuing & Selling Your Business*, 18.

43. Ibid., 15.

44. Les Nemethy, *Business Exit Planning*, 88.

45. Ibid., 88.

46. Ibid., 88.

47. Ibid., 89.

48. John F. Dini, *11 Things You Absolutely Need to Know About Selling Your Business*, 40.

49. Robert W. Scarlata, *Manage to Sell Your Business*, 90.
50. Fredrick D. Lipman, *The Complete Guide to Valuing & Selling Your Business*, 16.
51. Rick Rickertsen, *Sell Your Business Your Way*, 21.
52. James Allen, *As a Man Thinketh*, 30, 56-57.

Index